OUTSIDER available as a **GUIDE**

to

ANIMAL PRODUCTION

1995 Edition

JAN DE SMIT

Outsiders Guide

FOREWORD

ACKNOWLEDGEMENTS

The Publisher is grateful for the cooperation provided by all those sources listed under tables or charts within this publication.

In particular acknowledgement is given to:

Peter Hutchinson (The Agricultural Budgeting & Costing Book, Editions 38 and 39,1994) which has provided data used in most gross margin tables.

John Nix (Farm Management Pocket Book) for data used in fixed costs and field work rates data.

Meat and Livestock Commission for data used from their annual enterprise Year Books.

OUTSIDER'S GUIDE TO ANIMAL PRODUCTION 1995

Printed and bound by Da Costa Print, 35 - 37 Queensland Road, London N7 AH

II

OUTSIDER'S GUIDE TO ANIMAL PRODUCTION

THE OUTSIDER'S GUIDE SERIES

This is just one of the books in the Outsider's Guide series. There are three currently available. These are the Outsider's Guide to Crops, Animals and Horticulture.

The Outsider's Guides were specifically created to meet the need for concise, up-to-date information as a hand book. The Outsider's Guide provides key information about an enterprise in an easy to use and readily accessible layout.

This series is for all those who have not been involved in agriculture on a day to day basis but are about to be, or those that occasionally need to understand the nature of the business of farmers and growers.

Many people from many professions are using the Outsider's Guide. These are bank staff, accountants, agricultural students, journalists, loss adjusters, sales staff of agricultural suppliers, tax inspectors and advisory staff.

The series is an essential reference for every professional providing services to farmers and growers in the United kingdom.

THE OUTSIDER'S GUIDE TO ANIMAL PRODUCTION

The Outsider's Guide to Animal Production provides a concise guide to the main features of the seven main livestock enterprises on British Farms today. Each livestock enterprise is presented following the same easy-to-follow layout in eight sections.

You are introduced to the enterprise through an overview of production in the UK and the European Union. Interesting comparisons between member states are made and the main trends are illustrated. A novel benefit of this section is the list of key questions and performance indicators provided which enable you to assess a farmer's success.

Marketing is the key to any successful business and the factors which influence this are considered in this section, from product quality to market outlets and prices.

After setting the scene in this way, the Outsider's Guide then takes you logically through the husbandry of each livestock enterprise illustrating and explaining the nature of the decisions that the farmer has to make.

Naturally enough, this starts with a look at the best breeds and systems appropriate to the farm's location and intended market. Feeding, health, housing and reproduction of livestock are summarised in the subsequent four sections, before all these elements are brought together in 'Performance'. This will provide you with a summary of how a animal enterprise performs financially, and provides you with an indication of margins and overhead (investment) costs.

The Outsider's Guide to Animal Production concludes with two sections. These are a resume of the Common Agricultural Policy support for each livestock enterprise and finally some useful references, contacts and a glossary of terms used in animal production.

OUTSIDER'S GUIDE TO ANIMAL PRODUCTION

CONTENTS

OUTSIDER'S GUIDE TO ANIMAL PRODUCTION

CONTENTS

NOTES

THE
OUTSIDER'S GUIDE
to
BEEF

1995 Edition

OUTSIDER'S GUIDE

INTRODUCTION

World Production Of Meat

The total cattle population of the world is 1,284,870,000. There are 2 main types: European - developed from *Bos Taurus* and Zebu or hump-backed, developed from *Bos Indicus*. The latter are found in Asia and Africa. They were domesticated about 5000 BC and until the 18th century were mainly used for draught purposes. Today only about half are used for beef and milk.

Europe

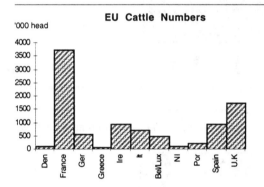

'000 head

EU Cattle Numbers

Total cattle numbers for the whole of Europe is 115 million. Nearly half of these are in the EU. The total number of beef cows in the EU. is about 8,180,000 head (1991). The number of beef cows in Holland is negligible.

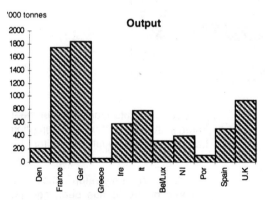

'000 tonnes

Output

The discrepency between the number of beef cows and beef production is accounted for mainly by beef produced from the dairy herd.

Source: M.L.C. Handbook 1994

PRODUCTION

Consumption

Consumption varies from 24.2kg/head in France to 12.7kg/head in Spain.

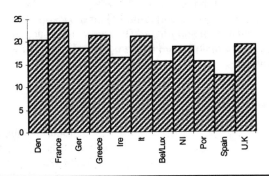

Consumption (kg/head)

UK

Since the advent of milk quotas, the UK dairy herd has declined in numbers with a concomitant increase in beef cattle.

1993 Breeding cows ('000):	4,517
dairy	2,772
beef	1,745
1993 Heifers in calf ('000):	813
dairy	576
beef	237

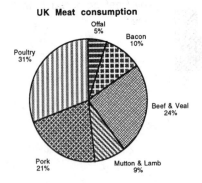

UK Meat consumption

Offal 5%
Bacon 10%
Poultry 31%
Beef & Veal 24%
Pork 21%
Mutton & Lamb 9%

Beef accounted for 24.2% of meat eaten in the UK in 1993. Consumption has remained relatively static for the past 5 years at about 19.5kg/head/yr.

Less beef is now eaten in the home but this decrease has been counter balanced by an increase in consumption in restaurants and hotels. An increasing % of beef is now used in convenience foods rather than traditional roasts.

OUTSIDER'S GUIDE

Self Sufficiency

Home production is now 96% of consumption and has seen a fall from 1984 when the UK was 111% self sufficient. The reduction of dairy herd numbers has contributed to this state, because a large proportion of UK beef is a by-product of the dairy herd (55%).

	Home production ('000 tonnes)	Home production as % of total supplies
1983	1,046	100
1984	1,152	111
1985	1,148	102
1986	1,062	94
1987	1,099	95
1988	947	86
1989	959	99
1990	1,001	100
1991	1,019	102
1992	959	96
1993	888	93

Source: M.L.C. Review 1993

Distribution Of Holdings

Beef production accounts for 17% of overall farm income. The distribution of producers is nationwide. Rearing is the predominant aspect in the upland areas and fattening in the lowland areas. Since 1950 many farms in the intensive arable areas of East England have replaced their beef units. In 1974, 78,000 holdings had beef cows, the average number being only 16.6 cows. Since that time, herds have become bigger and holdings keeping them have been reduced. In 1993 there were 73,000 holdings, 25% keeping between 50-100 cows each.

Prices

Beef prices show a small inverse relationship with numbers of cattle. Higher beef prices usually lead to an increase in poultry and pork consumption. Both of these have increased their market penetration in recent years.

PRODUCTION

FACTORS AFFECTING PROFITABILITY

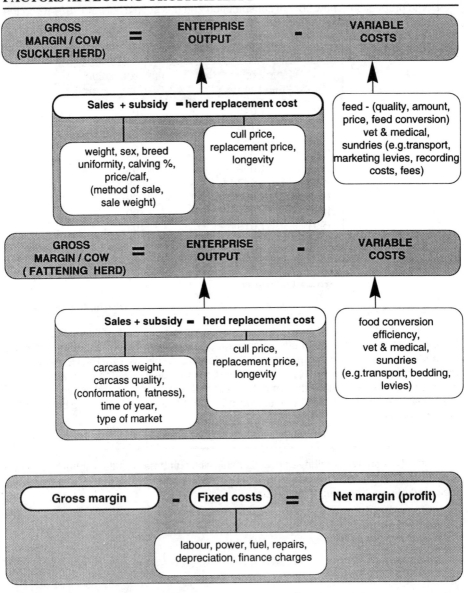

| GROSS MARGIN / COW (SUCKLER HERD) | = | ENTERPRISE OUTPUT | - | VARIABLE COSTS |

Sales + subsidy – herd replacement cost

weight, sex, breed uniformity, calving %, price/calf, (method of sale, sale weight)

cull price, replacement price, longevity

feed - (quality, amount, price, feed conversion) vet & medical, sundries (e.g.transport, marketing levies, recording costs, fees)

| GROSS MARGIN / COW (FATTENING HERD) | = | ENTERPRISE OUTPUT | - | VARIABLE COSTS |

Sales + subsidy – herd replacement cost

carcass weight, carcass quality, (conformation, fatness), time of year, type of market

cull price, replacement price, longevity

food conversion efficiency, vet & medical, sundries (e.g.transport, bedding, levies)

Gross margin – **Fixed costs** = **Net margin (profit)**

labour, power, fuel, repairs, depreciation, finance charges

THE PRODUCTION CYCLE

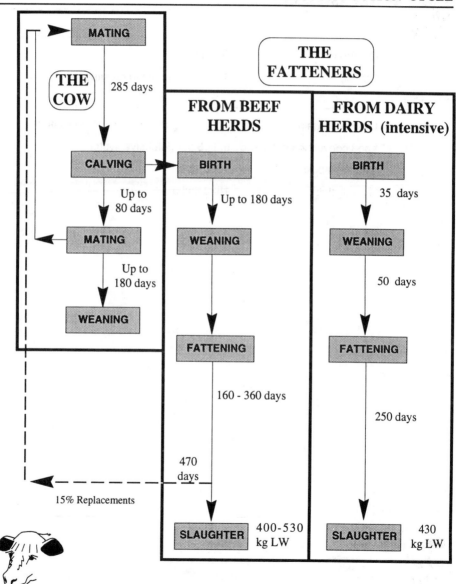

PRODUCTION

 KEY ASSESSMENT QUESTIONS

Rearing

Calving index	365 days
Calving %	91-96% depending on situation

Fattening

Liveweight gain	0.9 - 1.3 kg/day depending on system
Food conversion efficiency	5.0 - 5.5:1 (intensive system)
Grazing stocking rate	1500 kg/ha
Overall stocking rate	1800 kg/ha

MARKETING

PRODUCTS

Veal from calves fed milk-based diets and giving a carcass of 100-160 kg.

Beef

    i   from steers, maiden heifers and young bulls, known as clean beef

    ii   from cows and old bulls

Beef from the former is mainly sold as joints with only a small proportion being diverted to manufactured products (sausages, pies etc.). Beef from other animals is often diverted to manufacture.

1	Shin of beef	
2	Rounds	
3	Aitch bone	
4	Rump	
5	Sirloin	
6	Three rib	
7	Six rib	
8	Chuck	
9	Clod	
10	Brisket	
11	Flank	
12	Thick flank	

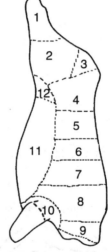

Reared calves are either 5-10 months old from the suckler herd, weighing 250-350 kg, or 5 or 12 week old artificially reared calves from the dairy herd weighing 65 and 100 kg respectively.

Stores are growing animals of varying ages and weights and are often transferred to another farm for fattening.

MARKET OUTLETS

Weaned calves from the suckler herds and stores are usually sold through auction markets. Many dairy bred calves are sold through calf dealers. Fat cattle are either sold live through auction markets or direct to abattoirs. The latter has become more popular in recent years and now accounts for more than 50% of fat cattle sold. Only a few auction markets are capable of handling young bulls.

OUTSIDER'S GUIDE

MARKETING

There has been an increase in fattening bulls rather than steers since prejudice declined and now 18% of clean cattle are bulls. This gives distinct economic benefits - higher liveweight gain, better food conversion efficiency and a better (leaner) carcass.

Prices for calves and stores are usually higher when beef prices are high.

Finished Cattle

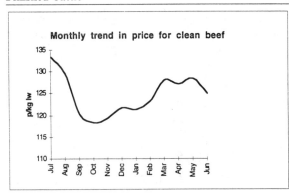

For fat cattle, there is a small seasonal price variation which basically follows the number coming forward. The trough usually is in October, when many animals are coming fat off grass and the peak in May and June when nothing is coming fat off grass.

Source: Farmers Weekly 1994

Average Monthly Prices For Store Steers

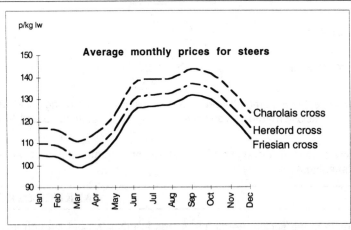

Source: M.L.C. 1993

Monthly prices for store heifers are lower because of lower potential growth rates.

Average market price for slaughter cattle (p/kg lw)

January	125	July	124
February	120	August	118
March	122	September	117
April	128	October	115
May	127	November	116
June	125		

Source: M.L.C. 1993

Besides supply and demand the carcass quality is the big determinant of price.

QUALITY

M.L.C. Classification Scheme

Conformation refers to the shape of the carcass. A convex shape is desired. A good conformation is significant to the butcher in giving more of the expensive cuts. Continental breeds and their crosses tend to give a better conformation than Friesians and Holsteins.

Fat class 1 is undesirable as there is an insufficient fat cover to stop the meat drying out when cooked. Classes 5L and 5H are too fat for almost all markets and the demand for class 4H is lessening.

Percentage distribution of clean beef carcasses in the classification grid for Great Britain, 1993:

CONFORMATION CLASS	FAT CLASS — Increasing Fatness							
	1	2	3	4L	4H	5L	5H	Overall
E			0.1	0.1				0.2
U+		0.1	0.4	0.6	0.2			1.4
-U		0.4	2.1	3.9	1.7	0.2		8.4
R	0.1	1.1	7.5	18.8	8.7	1.0	0.2	37.4
O+	0.1	1.1	7.7	17.2	7.4	1.0	0.3	34.7
-O	0.1	0.9	4.2	6.5	2.8	0.6	0.1	15.2
P+		0.3	0.8	0.7	0.2	0.1		2.1
-P	0.1	0.1	0.1	0.1				0.5
Overall	0.5	4.2	22.9	47.9	21.0	2.9	0.6	

(Improving Conformation ↑)

Source: M.L.C. Beef Yearbook 1993

MARKETING

Other quality factors include colour (a dark colour is selected against); fat colour (white fat is desired) tenderness and flavour (the latter two are mutually exclusive).

Payments

Abattoirs publish the basis of payment. For carcasses between specified weights a base-price is stated with premiums and deductions for carcasses with better or worse quality than the standard.

Beef Pricing Grid

Steers	260 - 320 kg carcass weight
Heifers	195 - 260 kg carcass weight
Bulls	235 - 300 kg carcass weight

The base price is quoted weekly.

	1	2	3	4L	4H	5L	5H
E	+12	+12	+12	+12	B		
U+	+6	+6	+6	+6	A		
-U	+6	+6	+6	+6	S		
R		BASE			E		
					-6		
O+	-10	-4	-4	-4	-8		
-O	-18	-12	-12	-12	-18		
P+							
-P							

Weights and grades not specified are paid for on a realisation basis.

All weight and classification data is recorded by the M.L.C. or other statutory levies, will be deducted at the appropriate rate.

Source: Barrett and Baird Ltd

Auction market prices reflect the expected carcass conformation, fatness and killing out %. Heifers give a fatter carcass at similar weights compared to steers which in their turn, give a fatter carcass than bulls of the same weight.

As the fatness of steers increases, so the deadweight price decreases, but only by about 2 - 4 %.

MARKETING

Marketing Costs For Fat Cattle

M.L.C. levy

Slaughtering levy of £3.28 per animal of which £2.51/animal can be passed back to the producer.

Transport to abattoir/market.

Market charges for cattle sold liveweight are variable depending on particular markets e.g. 1.5% of sale price (Grantham).

MARKETING

BREEDS & SYSTEMS

Modern breeds have been developed through in-breeding of selected cattle.

MAIN BREEDS IN U.K.

Native

i   For hill situations - Galloway, Aberdeen Angus, Welsh Black, Blue Grey (Galloway x White Beef Shorthorn). These breeds are hardy and have low maintenance requirements (i.e. low liveweight).

ii   For lowland situations - Hereford, Lincoln Red, Devon, Sussex, South Devon. These breeds are bigger and hence, have higher maintenance requirements. The South Devon gives more milk than the others.

Imported

Charolais, Simmental, Limousin, Belgian Blue, Blonde d'Aquitaine, Murray Grey.

These are large breeds with high maintenance requirements and increased calving difficulties. They are later maturing i.e. put down fat later in life compared to native breeds. This, allied to good carcass conformation, makes for good carcass quality. They also have a better liveweight gain/day.

Cross breeding is normal. As so many beef cattle come from the dairy herd, almost all of them are Friesian crosses. Many suckler cows too are Friesian crosses. The Friesian calf is used for beef as a pure-bred. It is later maturing and tends to produce a poor conformation carcass.

BREED IMPROVEMENT

Mainly through young bull testing. On-farm performance tests are done on either an individual or co-operative basis to compare young bulls under similar management for growth rate - a fairly highly heritable factor, and other desirable characteristics.

Traits	
Post-weaning growth rate	Yearling weight
Feed conversion efficiency	Subcutaneous fat thickness
Eye muscle area	

Source: Preston and Willis (1970) Intensive Beef Production. Pergammon Press,Oxford, England.

Backfat scanning is performed at the end of the test.

BLUP (Best Linear Unbiased Prediction)

This system enables genetic comparisons and is based on year 1980. It evens out seasons, years, management and farm influences on growth. It uses E.B.V.'s (estimated breed values) for backfat depth and muscling scores.

BREEDS & SYSTEMS

Breeding Systems

For commercial beef production, cross breeding is the norm. This gives hybrid vigour - the greatest degree being given by a 3 way cross, i.e. cross bred cow x 3rd breed bull.

PRODUCTION SYSTEMS

Rearing

i **Single suckling** - the cow rears her own calf until weaning at 5 - 8 months. Calf quality is high - cow productivity low.

ii **Multiple suckling** - a dairy type cow rears her own plus several purchased calves - calf quality is lower but cow productivity greatly increased.

iii **Artificial rearing** - calves from the dairy herd are reared on milk and milk substitute with concentrates offered ad lib. Weaning takes place at 5-6 weeks.

Fattening

i **Intensive** - cattle from 12 weeks kept indoors on ad. lib. concentrates. The growth rate and concentrate prices and Calf Cost are the main determinants of profitability. Only suitable for males of later maturing breeds.

ii **Semi-intensive** (18 month beef) - based on grass, silage and limited amounts of concentrates. Most suited to autumn born calves. They spend first winter inside on ad lib silage and 2kg/day concentrates, graze during the succeeding summer and are then fattened on ad-lib silage and 2-4kg/day concentrates.

iii **Grass silage beef** - A 14-16 month system based on indoor feeding of silage with a limited (2kg/day) amount of concentrates. Returns per ha are very good if first quality silage is made.

iv **Store fattening** - this is either done in summer on grass or in winter in yards with a variety of feeding regimes. Profitability is largely dependent on store prices.

PRODUCTION TARGETS

Rearing

1 calf/cow/year in suckler herds. Calves 64kg at 6wks, 100 kg at 12 weeks on milk substitute systems.

Fattening

Intensive 230-260 kg carcass by 12 months
Semi-intensive 250-280 kg carcass by 20 months
Grass silage beef 250-280 kg by 15 months

NUTRITION

INTRODUCTION

Beef cattle are ruminants with four "stomachs". A huge population of microbes in two of them enables high fibre foods (roughage) to be digested.

Diets with high amounts of roughage (hay, straw and silage) produce low rates of gain. Where high rates of gain are required, extra energy must be given and this involves a substantial inclusion of cereals.

Cattle can utilise root crops (turnips, swedes, fodderbeet) succulents (kale, cabbage) and many by-products (sugar beet pulp, potatoes, carrots). The major food for most cattle in the summer is still grass.

KEY ASSESSMENT QUESTIONS

Food conversion efficiency (intensive system) 5.0 - 5.5:1

Liveweight gain intensive system 1.1 - 1.3 kg/day

semi intensive 0.9 kg/day

silage beef 1 - 1.1 kg/day

Heifers grow about 10% slower than steers which in turn, grow about 8% less than bulls.

GRAZING SYSTEMS

i   **Extensive**. This is traditional for sucklers and the fattening of summer stores. No attempt is made to adjust numbers to grass growth. The cattle stay on the same field for the season.

ii **Rotational.** This system is often used for semi-intensive systems. The cattle are moved round a limited number of paddocks. This often involves increasing the area by inclusion of silage areas later in the season.

Stocking Rates

i   Sucklers (lowland) 1.5 - 2.5 cows/ha
    Sucklers (hill)   1.1 - 2 cows/ha in-bye land
ii Fatteners semi intensive grazing 4-7/ha, overall 3.5-5/ha
    Fatteners silage beef 5.5-9/ha

Growth rates will suffer if beef cattle are expected to completely eat up. If drought occurs, a roughage supplement is most economic.

Silage Storage Costs (1994)

Silage clamp	timber side - £165/m² or	£41/t silage
	pre-cast concrete £210/m²	£80m²/t silage

Prices exclude effluent tank which is essential to prevent water pollution.

NUTRITION

FEEDING AIMS

Suckler Cows

Grass only in summer when body weight should increase. For spring calvers winter feeding at maintenance level only i.e. roughage. For autumn calvers fed to give maintenance and 1.5 gallons of milk i.e. roughages and 1-2kg/day cereals. The calves may be creep fed on concentrates. This is of doubtful economic benefit whilst at grass.

Growing And Fattening Cattle

Intensive

Ad lib feeding of cereals and protein/mineral/vitamin supplement in 85:15 ratio to 250kg L.W. and then 90:10 ratio. Food conversion efficiency worsens considerably in later stages. Maximum growth rate is achieved by this method 1.1 - 1.3kg/day depending on breed and whether entire or castrated.

Semi intensive

Maximum growth is required from the cheap grazing. First winter growth is not maximised to obtain compensatory growth at grass. Ad lib silage and a maximum of 2kg concentrates per day is fed in the first winter to give turn out L.W. of 180 kg. Finishing is on ad lib roughage and 2kg of concentrates per day rising to 4 kg for males of later maturing breeds.

Silage beef

First quality silage (D value 67-69) is fed throughout ad lib with 2kg concentrates/day to give a gain of 1-1.1kg/day.

 Ration Formulation

This is based on the metabolisable energy (M.E.).

Body weight (kg)	Daily appetite (kg dry matter)	Maintenence energy MJ M.E./day	% Crude protein in diet
100	2.94	17	16
200	5.48	27	
300	7.62	36	14
400	9.36	45	
500	10.70	54	12
600	11.65	63	

INTRODUCTION

A high health status is necessary to allow maximum expression of potential. Diseases which are sub-clinical can markedly lower productivity. As with other livestock the greater the degree of intensification the greater the disease risk.

For many cattle diseases a predisposing factor is needed before the disease is seen. Such factors include age, weather, nutrition, housing, stress.

SOME COMMON DISEASES

Metabolic

i Bloat

This occurs when there is insufficient fibre in the diet. The situations when this is likely are intensive cereal fattening systems and turn out in spring to lush grass. Methane is unable to escape from the rumen eventually putting pressure on the heart and stopping it.

ii Grass staggers

Usually this occurs at turn-out in spring but can occur in out-wintered suckled cows particularly at a time of bad weather. The mechanism which supplies magnesium to the blood fails causing nervousness, staggering, quickly leading to coma and death.

iii Acidosis

Sudden death due to high acidity in the blood as a result of animals gorging themselves on concentrates.

Nutritional

i Pine

A wasting condition due to lack of cobalt.

ii Muscular dystrophy

A vitamin E deficiency most likely on a straw and root diet. Hind limbs' muscles affected.

Bacterial

i Coliform scours

Common in artificially reared calves which have had insufficient colostrum. Leads to dehydration and death.

ii Salmonellosis

Again a calf disease characterised by scouring but with blood. Transmittable to man.

iii Pastuerellosis

One type of pneumonia giving a fever and rapid shallow breathing. Often fatal if not treated. Prevalent in badly ventilated buildings. Vaccination can be employed.

iv Mastitits

A disease of suckler cows where udder hardens and swells, reducing milk supply. In some cases the affected quarter may be completely destroyed.

Fungal

Ringworm

Destroys hair of face and causes crustation. Transmittable to men. Fungus lives in wood and therefore only lives in housed cattle.

Viral

i   Pneumonia

One of the commonest causes of death in housed cattle. Viral pneumonia is not cured by antibiotics.

ii Infectious bovine rhino tracheitis (I.B.R.)

Symptoms similar to pneumonia and generally seen in cattle over 6 months. Internally housed cattle at greatest risk.

iii Enzootic bovine leukosis (E.B.L.)

This virus causes leukemia and later gives tumours in the lymph system. It leads to wasting and death. This is a notifiable disease.

iv Foot and mouth disease

This gives blisters on tongue and feet, produces much salivation and a high temperature. The virus can be transmitted by wind and birds as well as by more usual routes. This is a notifiable disease.

Parasitic

Internal

i Husk

A parasite living in the respiratory tract causing breathing difficulties and wasting, particularly in young cattle. Usually occurs in Aug-Sept and only in grazed cattle. Vaccination before turn-out is very effective.

ii Gastro-enteritis

Various parasites live in intestinal tract producing reduced growth rates and scouring in grazing cattle or cattle that have been grazed.

iii Fluke

Adult lives in bile duct of liver impairing its function and leading to anaemia and loss of condition. A mud snail is required for part of the life-cycle and thus the condition is found in wet areas.

External

Warble fly larvae migrate to animals back and pierce skin to breathe. This is a notifiable disease.

General

Foot troubles and leg abscesses which are more frequent in cattle housed on slats.

NOTIFIABLE DISEASES

Certain diseases of cattle must by law be notified to the local Divisional Veterinary Officer or the police immediately they are suspected. Notifiable diseases of cattle are:-

Anthrax - blood discharge from the orifices, highly contagious.
Tuberculosis } have not occurred in the U.K. for
Cattle plague (rinderpest) } many years.
Contagious bovine pleuro-pneumonia
Enzootic bovine leukosis
Foot and mouth disease
Rabies
Brucellosis
Bovine Spongiform Encephalopathy

(Salmonellosis is also notifiable under the 'Zoonoses Order 1975.)

PREVENTION OF DISEASE

i Vaccination - Vaccines must be kept at 2°C - 8°C and two injections are required to give adequate immunity in most cases.

HEALTH

ii Isolation-of purchased breeding stock.

iii Pasture management - Young cattle must never follow older cattle when grazing, as older cattle acquire a certain immunity to parasites which young stock lack. The ideal is to graze land not grazed by cattle in previous year. Normally drugs are required from July for grazed cattle to keep down their burden.

iv Housing - Essential to have adequate ventilation.

v Nutrition - Important to provide magnesium supplements and dosage at critical times.

vi Hygiene - A very high standard required in rearing calves artificially.

Sources of Disease

Other cattle, pasture, environment.

LEGAL ASPECTS

Code for the use of medicines

i Source

Drugs may only be obtained from a vet, pharmacy or in some cases a registered merchant. Some drugs are only available on prescription.

ii Storage

They must be stored safely and not misused. Temperature and light can be critical. Some products must be kept under lock and key.

iii Withdrawal times

Withdrawal periods are laid down for specific products relating to the time between the end of treatment and the date of slaughter. It is important to avoid certain residues in meat for human consumption.

iv Records (Cattle Identification document 1993)

Records of disease treatment must be kept and also records of the purchases (date, quantity, stock). In some cases empty bottles must be returned to the supplier. Records of stock movements must be kept.

All animals need to have two approved identical eartags carrying the same i.d.. Applied 36hr - 7 days after birth. Detailed records must be kept and accompany the animal when sold. Kept for 10 years.

OUTSIDER'S GUIDE

SYSTEMS

In fattening straw and slurry based systems are employed. For calf rearing on the artificial system individual or group pens are used.

REQUIREMENTS

Temperature

Except for the very young calf low temperatures can be tolerated. This is due to the immense heat production from the rumen microbes.

Lower critical temperature for various classes of cattle in very low air movement conditions.

	Liveweight (kg)	Lower critical temperature (°C)
Calves - new born	40	+11
- one month old	65	+7
- veal (1.5kg D.L.W.G.)	100	-8
Young beef cattle (1.0kg D.L.W.G.)	150	-16
D.L.W.G. = Daily Liveweight Gain		

Source: A.J.F. Webster, N.A.C. Conference 1978

Ventilation

This is the most critical requirement to remove moisture, ammonia and microbes. Natural ventilation is quite adequate although some calf houses do employ fan-based systems.

Air Velocity

High velocities at stock levels (i.e. draughts) result in chilling and should be avoided particularly for calves.

Recommendations for temperature, air velocity and ventilation rate:

	Temperature range (°C)	Max. air velocity at stock level (m/s)	Ventilation per kg liveweight (m³/h)
Calves (all ages)	5 - 20	0.25	0.75 - 2.25
Finishing cattle (adult stock)	0 - 15	0.25	0.50 - 1.50

Source: British Standards BS5502

HOUSING

Humidity

High humidities encourage microbes. Good drainage of urine allied to good ventilation helps to keep humidity under control.

Noxious Gases

These may build up from stagnant urine or slurry. Maximum allowable gas concentrations:

Gas	Concentration for calves ppm(v/v)*	Concentration for adult cattle ppm(v/v)
Carbon dioxide	3000	5000
Ammonia	20	25
Hydrogen sulphide	5	10

* ppm = parts per million
v/v = volume for volume

Source: BS5502

Dry Bed

A high heat loss occurs from calves forced to lie on wet bedding as well as the effect on humidity.

Lying Space

Stocking rates on solid floors (m²/head)

Liveweight in kg	Bedding area* (excluding troughs)	Loafing/feeding area (exclud. troughs)	Total area*
200	2.0	1.0	3.0
300	2.4	1.0	3.4
400	2.6	1.2	3.8
500	3.0	1.2	4.2
600	3.4	1.2	4.6

* For fully bedded yards the total area should be used.

Source: BS5502

Recommendations for fully slatted floors:

Liveweight (kg)	Stocking rate (m²/beast) (exclud. troughs)	Minimum width of slat (mm)	Maximum width of gap (mm)
200	1.1	125	40
300	1.5	125	40
400	1.8	125	40
500	2.1	125	40
600	2.3	125	40

Source: BS5502

Suckler cows may be out-wintered but the land becomes badly poached and no food saving is achieved.

Housing and feeding requirements for suckler cows, suckled calves and rearing stock:

	Housing* (m² per head)		Feeding (mm trough space)	
	straw bedding	slats	Restricted feeding	Ad lib
Cows	5.0-6.0	3.0-3.5	600-700	140-175
Creep area	1.0-2.0	1.0	n/a	75
Suckled calves	3.5-4.0	1.5-1.8	450-550	110-140
Stores/finishing cattle	3.8-4.3	1.8-2.1	550-650	140-170

*Excludes feed troughs and feeding passages

Trough Space

Liveweight (kg)	Feeding frontage (mm/beast)	
	Rationed feeding	Ad lib feeding
130 - 250	300 - 450	100
250 - 350	450 - 550	125
over 350	550 - 700	150

Source: BS5502

HOUSING

Water

Consumption per head per day (litres)	Number of bowls per 20 beasts	Surface area of trough per 20 beasts (m²)
50	2	0.3

Source: A.D.A.S. Beef Cattle Housing.

Group Size

For fattening cattle this should not be too large. 20-25 is the maximum for bulls. Bulls from different pens should never be mixed.

CAPITAL COST

i   For concreted straw bedded yard with central drive-through passage having feed barriers alongside:

£112/m² per 300kg animal £470;   per 550kg animal £540.

ii   For slatted building with central drive through passage and slurry cellar beneath sufficient for 80 - 90 days supply:

£165/m² per 300kg animal £452;   per 550kg animal £528.

iii   Calf house for artificial rearing (40 places), individual pens and including food store:

£112/m² per calf place £310.

Systems which have cattle on the farm for two winters incur substantial extra capital in buildings.

WASTE DISPOSAL SYSTEM

The straw bedding is added daily and allowed to build up until the pen is cleared. It is then handled as a solid and spread over the land.

Slurry production increases with age, and often needs removing several times during the fattening period. This is usually done by a tanker.

Liveweight(kg)	Approximate volume of waste/head (litres/day)* (faeces + urine)
85 - 140	7
140 - 330	14
330 - 450	21
over 450	32

Source: BS5502

HOUSING

Pollution

With slurry care should be taken to avoid pollution of the air (housing estates), water courses and underground water collection areas. The addition of silage effluent to slurry can be dangerous.

LEGAL REQUIREMENTS

Under the Agriculture (Miscellaneous Provisions) Act 1986 a welfare code operates whose basic provisions are:

comfort and shelter

readily accessible fresh water and a diet to maintain the animals in full health and vigour

freedom of movement

the company of other animals

the opportunity to exercise most normal patterns of behaviour

natural light during the hours of daylight and artificial lighting readily available to enable the animals to be inspected at any time

flooring which neither harms the animals or causes undue strain

the prevention or rapid diagnosis and treatment of vice, injury, parasitic infestation and disease

the avoidance of unnecessary mutilation

emergency arrangements to cover outbreaks of fire, the breakdown of essential mechanical services and the disruption of supplies.

The code draws attention to situations in which welfare could be placed at risk and suggests measures which can be taken to avoid this.

Legislation

Control of Pollution Act 1974 prohibits discharge or seepage of farm wastes into watercourses or ground water extracted for human consumption.

The Town and County Planning Order 1988 requires that specific planning permission must be obtained where :

i   the ground area of new or extended building exceeds 465 m. This figure includes any adjacent building work over the last 2 years

ii   the height of any part of the building work exceeds 3m, is within 3km of the perimeter of an aerodrome

HOUSING

iii the height of any part of the building work exceeds 12 m

iv any part of the work would be within 25 m of a trunk/classified road

v the construction is for the accommodation of livestock or the storage of slurry/sewage within 400 m of certain 'protected' buildings where people live or work. (The main farmhouse and farm workers cottages are outside the meaning of "protected" building.)

REPRODUCTION

KEY ASSESSMENT QUESTIONS

For lowland suckler herds:

Age at first calving	2 years
Calving period	9 weeks
Calves reared/cow/year	1
Calf weight gain	1kg/day
Age at sale/transfer	263 days
Weight at sale/transfer	293 kg
Stocking rate	1.9 cows/ha

Lower stocking rates are acceptable in upland situations.

KEY FACTS

Heat (oestrus) cycle

Cycle length	20 - 21 days average. Range 18 - 24 days
Duration	average 18 hours. Range 6 (winter) - 24 hours
Ovulation occurs	10 - 12 hours after end of heat period
Ovulation rate	1 egg
Insemination	6 - 24 hours after beginning of heat

Service in suckler herds is usually natural with 1 mature bull to 50 cows, 1 young bull to 30 cows.

Artificial insemination is possible and most frequently done for heifers after hormonal treatment to synchronise heat. It is usually done by Genus.

The bull should not run with the cows for more than nine weeks to concentrate calving period and ease management.

Cows should be on rising plane of nutrition at service or with a body condition score of 2.5 otherwise conception is reduced.

Confirmation of pregnancy is normally carried out by rectal palpation 40 - 59 days after service.

OUTSIDER'S GUIDE

REPRODUCTION

CALVING

The gestation period averages 284 days with heavier breeds having a longer period.

Calving may be indoors or out, the latter giving less disease problems but making it more difficult to render assistance if necessary.

The heavier breeds tend to have a greater number of calving difficulties and higher calf mortality, although there is a considerable variation between bulls within a breed.

Sire breed	Assisted calvings (%)	Calf mortality (%)	Calving interval (days)	Annual production of calf weaning weight per cow (kg)
Charolais	9.0	4.8	374	208
Simmental	8.9	4.2	374	203
South Devon	8.7	4.0	375	203
Devon	6.4	2.6	373	200
Limousin	7.4	3.8	375	199
Lincoln red	6.7	2.0	373	198
Sussex	4.5	1.5	372	196
Hereford	4.0	1.6	372	189
Angus	2.4	1.3	370	179

Source: M.L.C. Blueprint for suckler beef.

Calving can be arranged at any season. Spring calving has low concentrate requirements, few problems getting cows in-calf but by autumn has only produced a lightweight calf. Autumn/winter calving involves much higher concentrate usage, creates more difficulties in reproduction but gives a big calf for sale.

The worst situation from a managerial and profitability point of view is all the year round calving.

Reproduction Improvements

i   Bull performance testing.

ii Embryo transfer. This technique involves drug treatment of a superior cow to produce many eggs which are fertilised and then flushed out and implanted in other cows which have been synchronised for their heat cycles with the donor.

iii Establishment of a Cow Index to mark relative merits of cows.

PHYSICAL PERFORMANCE

KEY ASSESSMENT QUESTIONS

Lowland Suckler Herd

Calving interval	365 days
Calving percentage	95%
Stocking rate	2 - 2.5 cows/ha
Replacement rate	15%

Fattening - Semi-Intensive

Liveweight gain	1st winter 0.8kg/day
Weight at turnout	180kg
Liveweight gain at grazing	0.9kg/day
Weight at yarding	340kg
Liveweight gain	2nd winter 0.8-0.9kg/day

Fattening - Intensive

Liveweight gain	1.1 - 1.3kg/day
Food conversion efficiency	100-250kg L.W. 4:1 F.C.E.
	250kg upwards 6:1 F.C.E.
	Overall 5 - 5.5:1 F.C.E.

Calf Rearing   12 week weight - 100kg.

GROSS MARGINS

These are mainly dependent on the physical performance, carcass quality, calf price and concentrate costs.

PERFORMANCE

Lowland Beef Sucklers - Autumn Calving

Per cow	£
Sales 365kg calf x 91% reared @ 126p/kg	
liveweight (Autumn sale)	419
subsidy - EU suckler cow	87
Less depreciation - cow over 7 years,	
plus bull & calf replacement	68
OUTPUT	437
Variable costs	
Concentrates cow 225kg @ 13p/kg	27
calf 175kg @ 15p/kg	24
Bulk feed purchased	18
Vet & medical	20
Bedding 0.8 t straw	20
Variable sundries	20
VARIABLE COSTS (excluding forage costs)	124
GROSS MARGIN before forage	313
Forage costs: 0.56ha @ £108/ha	61
GROSS MARGIN after forage (£335/ha)	252

Source: A.B.C.

EU subsidy = £65.73/cow

Depreciation: replacement heifer at £800; average cull price of £475: 4% calves purchased at £155.

Lowland Beef Sucklers - Spring Calving

Per cow		£
Sales	280kg calf x93% reared @ 133p/kg	
	liveweight (autumn sale)	346
	subsidy - EU suckler cow	87
Less depreciation - cow over 7 years,		
	plus bull & calf replacement	61
OUTPUT		373
Variable costs		
Concentrates cow 125kg @ 13.5p/kg		17
	calf 60kg @ 17p/kg	10
Bulk feed purchased		20
Vet & medical		18
Bedding	0.6 t straw	15
Variable sundries		10
VARIABLE COSTS (excluding forage costs)		90
GROSS MARGIN before forage		283
Forage costs; 0.45ha @ £105/ha		48
GROSS MARGIN after forage		235

Source: A.B.C.

EU subsidy = £56/cow

Depreciation: Replacement heifer at £800; average cull of price £475: 4% calves purchased at £155.

PERFORMANCE

Gross Margin Trends (£ per head)

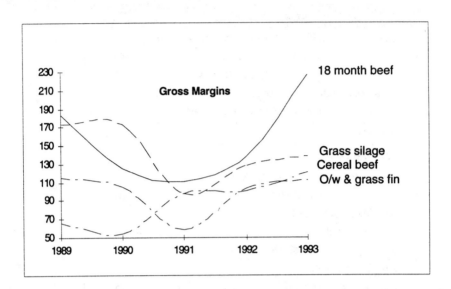

Fixed Costs

These vary enormously, largely depending on whether depreciation, interest and loan repayments have been incurred by erection of new buildings.

Labour in suckler and fattening system is about 9 - 12 hours/animal/year.

PERFORMANCE

PRICE SUPPORT

Intervention, Monetary Compensatory Allowances And Trade Agreements

Intervention is designed to take beef off the market when prices fall below a certain price. The EU will buy the beef and store it until prices improve.

Monetary compensatory allowances are designed to iron out distortions in currency rates between member states in the EU Intervention to be cut by 5% a year for 3 years.

Beef Special Premium (BSP)

Support paid directly to producers and is restricted to 90 male animals (at 10 and 22 months old) per year, when the animal is presented for slaughter. The payment is currently £56.34 (1993), £69.07 in 1994 and £82.89 in 1995 per animal and is claimed in two payments, the first payment being 60% of the total.

Suckler Cow Premium (SCP)

An annual headage payment including milk producers producing below 120,000kg of milk (up to 10 animals). Animals must be kept for six months from the date the claim for S.C.P is lodged.

There is one rate:

1994   £87.49
1995   £110.52

The payment is based on a suckler cow qouta and is based on premiums paid during 1992. These qouta's are transferable but 15% will go into a national reserve, no compensation is given. Leasing is allowed for a minimum of 1 year.

Hill Livestock Compensatory Allowances

These are paid at 2 levels to farmers in disadvantaged areas. The higher level on the more marginal (hill) farms £47.50 per cow and the lower level on somewhat more congenial situations, £23.75 per cow.

Integrated Administrative & Control System (I.A.C.S.)

Anti fraud measure to stop fraudulent claims for grants. I.A.C.S. applies to Arable Area Payments, Beef Special Premium and Suckler Cow Premium. The system involves a form filling exercise which includes the submission of O.S. maps to M.A.F.F. for identification purposes.

Other parts of the system will comprise of an identification system for each field, a system for identification and registration of certain animals. Penalties for late and inaccurate applications are severe.

PERFORMANCE

THE
OUTSIDER'S GUIDE
to
BROILERS

1995 Edition

OUTSIDER'S GUIDE

POULTRY PRODUCTION

The Poultry Meat Industry in the UK comprises of the following product sectors:

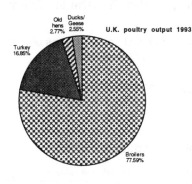

U.K. poultry output 1993

1 Broiler chicken accounts for the largest share of the sector.

2 Broiler production in the UK started to increase in the 90's. Total UK production 1993 being some 838,000 tonnes less then 1992. However, the latter was achieved using 5 million less birds.

In terms of self-sufficiency the UK is a net importer of poultry meat, although the EU 12 are net exporters of Poultry meat. The UK market for Broiler meat is at present oversupplied with much cheap chicken arriving from non EU Countries. Thus the market and prices are depressed.

Consumption and production of broiler chicken meat increased slightly from 1992 - 1993.

	1989	1990	1991	1992	1993
Broilers	700,000	770,000	837,000	837,000	838,000
Turkeys	177,000	170,000	174,000	172,000	182,000
Old Hens	45,000	38,000	37,000	32,000	30,0000
Ducks/Geese	19,000	25,000	24,000	28,000	28,000

Sources: Poultry World 1994

The outlook for 1994-95 is not very good. The UK industry is rapidly heading for over production. The promises from GATT have not materialised and there is a threat of imports of non EU countries.

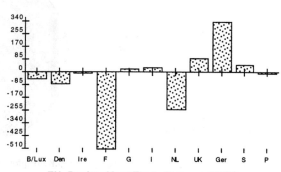

EU Poultry Meat Trade Balance ('000t)

PRODUCTION

UK Broiler Production

UK Broiler Production in 1993 was valued at about £1047m in contrast to egg production output at about £405m.

The National Broiler flock has increased over the past years in terms of tonnage but 1993 saw a slight decline with output falling some 8000 tonnes on 1992.

The number of units has decreased whilst the size of the unit has increased. In 1993 59.41% of UK Broilers were produced on units in excess of 100,000 bird size.

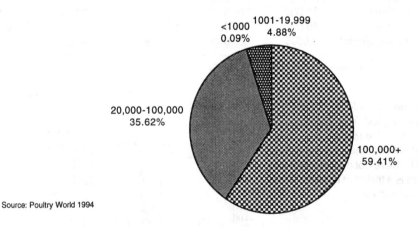

Source: Poultry World 1994

% of U.K. broiler units by size of flock

PRODUCTION

Production

The national flock is mainly housed intensively.

Some retail outlets have demanded slightly different products, and producers have fulfilled the demand by supplying:

> **Free Range broilers**
>
> **Corn fed broilers**
>
> **Additive-free broilers**

But these are only a small percentage of total production. While the outlook looked very promising in the late 1980's the recession has depressed demand in the 1990's.

Normal broiler chickens are grown for 42-49 days and achieve an average live weight of 1.9-2.3 kg. There is a demand for larger birds and thus males are grown on to 57-70 days to produce what is known as superchicken with live weights up to 3.8 kg.

The females are slaughtered at 42 days as they are inefficient to grow on much longer.

Consumption

Broiler meat consumption in the UK has increased over the last 12 years from 10.1 kg/head in 1981 - 14.7 kg/head in 1993 and is now stable.

Consumption of Broiler meat - UK (kg per head)
Source: Poultry World 1994

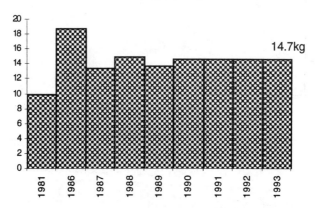

PRODUCTION

Some of the reasons for the increase in the consumption are because poultry meat is:

> ☞ **Recognised as a healthy food**
>
> ☞ **Very convenient in further processed forms**
>
> ☞ **Cheap**

Unlike the egg industry, the meat industry never really suffered from the salmonella scare, although poultry meat is often blamed for being the source of salmonella infections.

In general Broiler farmers have had a better time than the egg producers. The returns are nearer to the production costs. The turnover is quicker. One flock of broilers every 8 weeks as opposed to 52 weeks for an egg laying flock.

Quarterly Comparison of Prices Received and Costs

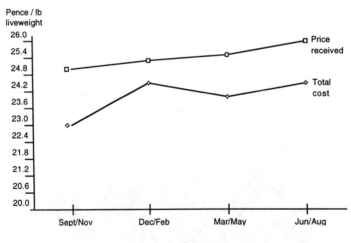

Source: NFU 1993

PRODUCTION

KEY ASSESSMENT QUESTIONS

Flock length	42 days	49 days
Average liveweight kg	1.94	2.37
Food consumed kgs	3.55	4.67
Food conversion ratio (FCR)	1.82:1	1.97:1
Food cost pence/kg	18.5	18.5
% Mortality	4.5	5.5
Price received pence/kg	58.4	58.4
Total Price pence received	113.29	138.40
Gross margin/bird pence	26.69	31.01
Stocking Density kg/m²	34.00	34.00
Returns/bird space p/yr.	173.9	179.54
Gross margin £/m²	4.67	4.44
Gross margin £/m²/yr.	30.48	25.74
Chick cost pence	21	21

The above is calculated from production figures produced by the breeding companies and using standard stocking densities. The stocking densities are laid down in the **Recommendations for the Codes of Welfare**.

If birds are housed more densely growth may be slowed down but more birds would be housed/m².

The above figures give a gross margin but refer to the Gross Margins in the Performance Section (🐥) which will establish the true picture and the actual profit figure.

PRODUCTION

FACTORS AFFECTING PROFITABILITY

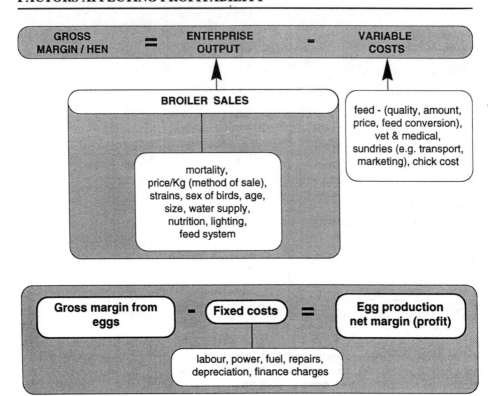

| GROSS MARGIN / HEN | = | ENTERPRISE OUTPUT | − | VARIABLE COSTS |

BROILER SALES

mortality,
price/Kg (method of sale),
strains, sex of birds, age,
size, water supply,
nutrition, lighting,
feed system

feed - (quality, amount,
price, feed conversion),
vet & medical,
sundries (e.g. transport,
marketing), chick cost

| Gross margin from eggs | − | Fixed costs | = | Egg production net margin (profit) |

labour, power, fuel, repairs,
depreciation, finance charges

Notes:

Price received/kg can vary from 58.4p - 60.6p. The former is about current production cost. For 'superchicken' the price needs to be about 2.25p/kg higher. The break even is about 54p/kg.

Sex of birds (cockerels) convert better and grow faster (pullets) convert worse and grow slower. **Age/size** The older birds or the bigger the greater their maintenance requirement before growth takes place giving poorer food conversion ratios.

Food cost. Food represents about 75% of production costs.

Scale of production - Larger units run more efficiently.

MARKETING

MAIN PRODUCT

There is only one product - live broiler chicken. These are sold under contract to the packer who processes and markets the product.

The processor may well produce further products from the broiler chicken and many do end up as burgers, nuggets, portions, kievs as well as the traditonal whole chicken.

Broilers are grown to various ages ranging from small 21 day chickens destined for a poussin market, to the heavy 70 day chicken. In the past males were castrated and sold as capons. This is now illegal and heavy birds are referred to as 'Superchicken' or 'Roasters'.

Broilers are either grown on company-owned farms or grown under contract.

The contract involves either:

> 1   the payment on crop completion on a pence/kg basis with bonus and penalty clauses for quality and quantity or
>
> 2   a price /m² for the house. In this case the processor would provide:
>
> **chick; feed; vet/med**
>
> and the contractor provides:
>
> **housing; labour; litter**

Normally two crops' notice are required to end the contract by either party.

Standards And Quality

There are five main products:

1	**Broiler**
2	**Superchicken**
3	**Free-range**
4	**Cornfed broiler**
5	**Additive-free broiler**

MARKETING

Product	Notes
1 Broiler	Grown to 42-49 days First quality penalties incurred for bruising, hock burns, breast blisters etc.
2 Superchicken	Grown 56 - 70 days First quality as above.
3 Free Range	Broilers as above generally grown to 56 days or more on reduced stocking densitites with access to range. Access to range is usually withheld until after 21 days. The quality requirements remain the same. Growth rate is slowed down to encourage a stronger carcase to enable the bird to range thus production costs are higher, however the returns are also much higher.
4 Cornfed broiler	As normal broilers but the bird is fed on a cereal based diet with further constraints. Same quality requirements expected, premium prices offered.
5 Additive-free Broilers	Small market but still being developed. Broilers fed on a diet that is free from growth promoters and coccidiostats (see disease 🔪section). It results in a slower growing bird but it commands a premium price. Over the years the killing age for broilers has fallen and the meat is now accused of being tasteless. Flavour can be improved by: **growing older birds** **hanging birds after killing but before evisceration**

It is questionable whether access to range or different diets will influence flavour.

Second grade broilers are of no value, they will not be accepted by the processor. They should therefore be culled out as they are found during the growing period.

INTRODUCTION

The type of chicken required for meat production is totally different to that used for Egg production.

The requirements for meat production are:

i	**fast growth**
ii	**efficient converter of food to meat**
iii	**high meat to bone ratio**
iv	**meat in the right places**
v	**white skin for UK market**
vi	**white feathers - makes processing easier**
vii	**high liveability**
viii	**high disease resistance**
ix	**high disease resistance**
x	**strong legs**

Broiler Breeding Companies

Pure breeds of Poultry are no longer used, nowadays special Broiler breeds are available.

There are about 6 companies available in the UK which produce stock . Stock is provided through franchised agents across the country. The breeds are all hybrids taking their name from the company which produced them - **COBB, ROSS, and HYBRO**.

COBB and ROSS are the market leaders accounting for nearly all the broilers in the UK at present. Other birds fail to meet the demands of the processor in one way or other.

Hatcheries

Broilers Parents are kept by most of the Integrated Companies and some independent Hatcheries. Hatching eggs are produced, hatched and the chicks sold to the broiler grower.

The source of chicks is normally tied into the contract under which the broilers are produced. Because broilers are hybrids none are retained beyond their normal killing age for breeding.

BREEDS & SYSTEMS

Alternative Systems

Whilst the majority of broilers are grown intensively there is a small market for birds reared on less extensive systems. These command a much higher price but must adhere to the following criteria* to qualify for their respective titles.

* set out by the EU

Alternative System

e.g. Corn-Fed Broilers

The ration must contain a minimum of 65% cereals; a maximum of 15% cereal by products; a maximum of 5% pulses or green vegetables; a maximum of 5% dairy products.

Extensive Indoor (Barn Reared)

Stocking Density of 12 birds/m² or 25 kg/m². Killing ages 56 days or later.

Free Range

Stocking density in the house 13 birds/m² or 27.7 kgs/m².

Birds to have continuous daytime access to grass runs or those covered with vegetation for at least half of their life. Area of run to be minimum of 1m²/chicken. Killing ages 56 days or later. The feed formula during fattening (ie after 3 weeks) to contain minimum of 70% cereals.

Popholes

There must be popholes, the combined length of which must be equal to or greater than the length of the long side of the house.

Traditional

Indoor stocking density is 12 birds/m2 or 25 kg/m².

Mobile house - max size 150m² remaining open at night - the stocking density should be 20 birds/m² or 40 kg/m²

For rearing "Capons"*:

6.25 birds/m² after 81 days of age or 12 birds/m² or 25 kg/m² for less than 81 days of age.

* Term "Capon" still used in the directive published in Official Journal of EU even though the practice is no longer allowed.

WATER

As with any livestock water is vital. It should be provided ad lib., and should be clean, fresh and easily accessible. Should water consumption be restricted feed intake will be reduced with a consequent reduction in growth rate.

Broilers are provided with water in one of the two kinds of drinking system.

1 Bell Drinkers

8 - 10 x 35cm diameter

Makes BEC (Broiler Equipment Company)

Rainbow Cavalier (Rainbow Valve Company)

Plasson

Bell drinker adjustment

These should be adjusted so that the lip of the drinker is as the height of the bird's back. The depth of water should be 2/3 - 3/4 full for the first 8-10 days and then reduced to 1 cm.

2 Nipple Drinkers/Cup Drinkers

1 nipple or cup to each 22 Broilers

Model	Maker
Aqua 2	Aqua 2 Products
Avicup	BEC

Nipple line adjustment

Nipple lines are set at a height requiring the bird to stretch to reach them. The bird then pecks the nipple and the water runs in its mouth and down its throat.

For the first few days the lines are set low and often incorporate a drip cup to catch spilt water.

A float attachment can be fitted to the nipple enabling the drip cup to fill with water to provide readily accessible water points for the day old chick.

NUTRITION

Cups

Normally these are set slightly above the chicks' back height.

Importance Of Correct Setting For Drinkers

Drinkers that are set incorrectly give poorer results.

Features	Consequences
Insufficient drinker points Raised too high Adjusted too shallow	Poor growth, possibly increased mortality
Too low Adjusted too deep	Wet litter, poor environment Disease downgrading

Which Is Best?

Nipple drinkers in broiler houses are a relatively new idea. Many makes are available, the best are very good, some are unreliable.

Nipple drinkers

1 are more hygienic - there being no water exposed to poultry house environment
2 do not require cleaning
3 are easier to manage
4 give better litter and therefore less degrading
5 may give slightly reduced growth rates.

Whilst point 5 is a disadvantage it is far outweighed by point 4.

Bell drinkers

Still very popular and serviceable but have a limited future as labour costs rise. In addition to this some of the big retail outlets are now demanding nipple lines in order to maximise hygiene in the flock.

NUTRITION

Supplementary drinkers

In addition to the nipple lines or the Bell drinkers installed in a poultry house, water is supplied in supplementary drinkers for the first 5-6 days.

These supplementary drinkers may be in the form of glass, plastic or galvanised steel founts, apple grays or plastic egg trays. They are used to ensure all chicks find water in the first days of life. In the warm environment of the brooding area the chicks can dehydrate very rapidly. Ideally they **need to find water within 6 hours** of being placed in the house.

FEEDING

Broiler chickens are fed using a quantitative programme. i.e. a quantity of starter diet followed by a quantity of grower diet etc.

Several programmes are available, different feed companies recommending different programmes.

All diets are fed in the form of crumbs for the starter and pellets for the rest.

Example: As Hatched Programme (A/H)

Diet	Quantity tonnes per1000	Approximate age range
Broiler Starter Crumbs ACS	0.275	0-10 days
Broiler Grower Pellets ACS	1.50	11-28 days
Broiler Finisher Pellets ACS Broiler Finisher Pellets (withdrawal) }	1,875 +	29 to kill (@ 42 days)

The rations contain an Anti Coccidia Supplement to aid in the prevention of coccidiosis. This must be removed from the diet for the last 3 or 5 days (depending on the drug used). When ordering food, withdrawal food is requested for use in this period.

To calculate the quantities required, charts are available listing food consumption at every age.

Most processors now require a written declaration stating that the birds have been fed a withdrawal ration for the last 3-5 days and records appertaining to that flock for number of birds reared, mortality etc.

NUTRITION

Diet Specification

Temperate region (<28°C operating temperature) A/H

		Starter	Grower	Finisher
CP	%	23	21	19.0
ME (MJ/kg)	%	12.97	13.38	13.68
Oil	%	4-7	4-9	4-9
Lysine	%	1.4	1.27	1.15
Methionine	%	0.65	0.60	0.57
M + C	%	0.93	0.84	0.76
Tryptophan	%	0.23	0.21	0.19
Calcium	%	1.00	0.90	0.80
Av. Phosphorous	%	0.45	0.45	0.35
Salt	%	0.32-0.36	0.34-0.36	0.36-0.38
Sodium	%	0.18-0.20	0.18-0.20	0.18-0.20
Chloride	%	0.16-0.18	0.17-0.19	0.16-0.18
Linoleic Acid	%	1.25 (min)	1.20 (min)	1.0(min)
Age fed days		0 to10	11 to 28	29 to process.

Source: Ross Breeders "Producing Quality Broiler meat"

Other rations are available for different classes of Broiler chicken.

Heavy Chicken Males Only

		Starter	Grower	Finisher 1	Finisher 2
CP	%	18	21	19.0	17.5
ME (MJ/kg)	%	11.92	13.20	13.38	12.97
Oil %	4-7	4-9	4-9	4-7	
Lysine	%	0.93	1.20	1.10	0.90
Methionine	%	0.4	0.59	0.55	0.45
M+C	%	0.72	0.95	0.86	0.77
Tryptophan	%	0.19	0.22	0.20	0.19
Calcium	%	0.90	0.90	0.90	0.90
Av. Phos	%	0.45	0.45	0.40	0.40
Salt	%	0.34	0.34	0.34	0.34
Sodium	%	0.15	0.15	0.15	0.15
Chloride	%	0.14	0.14	0.14	0.14
Linoleic Acid	%	1.10	1.30	1.20	1.00
Age fed days		0 to 14	15 to 28	29 to 42	42 to process
Kg/1000		750	1250	1500	1500

Source: Ross Breeders "Producing Quality Broiler meat"

NUTRITION

Broilers Where The Sexes Are Regraded And Fed Separately..

		Starter		Grower		Finisher	
		M	F	M	F	M	F
CP	%	23	23	21	20	19	18
ME (MJ/kg)	%	12.97	12.97	13.38	13.18	13.68	13.38
Oil	%	4-7	4-9	4-9	4-9	4-9	4-9
Lysine	%	1.4	1.4	1.27	1.21	1.15	1.09
Methionine	%	0.65	0.65	0.60	0.58	0.57	0.55
M+C	%	0.93	0.93	0.84	0.80	0.76	0.72
Tryptophan	%	0.23	0.23	0.21	0.20	0.19	0.18
Calcium	%	1.00	1.00	0.90	0.90	0.80	0.80
Av. Phos	%	0.45	0.45	0.45	0.45	0.35	0.35
Salt	%	0.32 to 0.36		0.34 to 0.36		0.36 to 0.38	
Sodium	%	0.18 to 0.20		0.1 to 0.20		0.18 to 0.20	
Chloride	%	0.16 to 0.18		0.17 to 0.19		0.16 to 0.18	
Linoleic Acid	%	1.25 mn		1.20 min		1.0 min	
Age fed days		0 to 10		11 to 28		29 to process	
Kg/1000		250	250	1500	1500	2000	1750

In general the females are fed a lower density diet.

The practice of rearing the sexes separately is on the increase for the following reasons

1   More even flock, enabling feeders and drinkers to be set more accurately.
2   More even bodyweights - makes processing easier.
3   More suitable diets can be fed to the respective sexes.

There are no pigments in Broiler diets and pigmented ingredients in the ration are avoided to prevent the carcase taking on a yellow appearance. In corn fed chicken the diet is based on maize, and the yellow pigment colours the carcase accordingly and it is a recognised feature of that product.

Storage

Food should be purchased in bulk and stored in bulk hoppers. Bagged food costs £15 to £20/tonne more and is susceptible to vermin damage. It also incurs an additional labour cost for double handling.

Food should be stored for the minimum period. Starter crumbs should run to a minimum before the grower pellet is put in the bin, otherwise the free flowing pellets will be used before all the crumbs are used up.

NUTRITION

Broiler diets contain a lot of fat and do not store very well, the fat or oil becoming oxidised in a relatively short time.

Pellets and crumbs are fed because they are more palatable than dry meal.

KEY FACTS

Daily food consumption A/H

Day	Grams	Day	Grams
1	12.5	28	103
7	30.8	35	129.5
14	70.0	42	146.5
21	88.6		

Total food consumption to 421 days A/H	3.625 kg
Body wt (average) to 42 days	1.940 kg
FCR	1.86:1

i.e 1.86 kg food is consumed to produce 1 kg of live weight.

Feed Requirements

Types of feeder available	Quantity required
Track and Chain Feeder	45 Broilers/m
Cable and Flight filled tubes	14 tubes/1000 birds
Pan Feeders	15 pans/1000 birds
Tube Feeders	30-40 tubes/1000

Auger in galvanised pipe

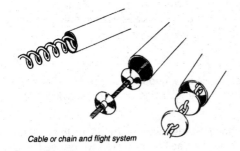

Cable or chain and flight system

Track and chain feeder system

NUTRITION

During the early brooding period the starter crumbs are placed in trays or on paper sheets as well as in the main feeding system. The chicks should have easy access. These supplementary feeders are removed after day 5-6.

Each system has its advantages and disadvantages.

	PAN FEEDERS	TUBES & TRACKS	CHAIN FEEDERS
Adjustment	adjustable from a single point, but every pan in the house needs adjusting if these systems are used.	may need to be raised from many points, but every tube in the house needs adjusting if these systems are used.	Feed level adjustment much easier with chain feeder - only one adjustment.
Food distribution	Distribute food to all feed points simultaneously with little damage to the pellet.		Chain feeders and cable and flight take longer and may cause the pellet to crumble.
Wastage	Pans waste less feed than tubes and chain feeders if adjusted correctly. a small % saving in food wastage represents a lot of money.	Waste more than pan feeders if adjusted correctly	Waste more than pan feeders if adjusted correctly
Downgrading	Less downgrading with pans because there are no moving parts.	Less downgrading with tubes because there are no moving parts.	More downgrading because of the moving parts
Labour		Hand filled tube feeders have a very high labour requirement.	

Whichever type is used - the lip of the feeder should be raised level with the birds back.

Chick Quality

In order to perform to their potential it is important that the chicks are of top quality when they arrive.

On placing the chicks check the following:

1 Numbers total with invoice - count number of chicks in boxes at random.
2 The chicks should be of equal size.
3 Active and bright
4 Fluffy - with no shell or yolk stuck to down.
5 There should be no deformities such as cripples or cross beaks.
6 They should feel firm - not hard (dehydrated) or soft (weak)
7 The navels are healed
8 There should be no dead on arrival.

The chicks should be inspected, the house temperature, delivery lorry temperature and any other comments should be recorded on the delivery note before signing for receipt.

NUTRITION

Broiler Diseases

Broilers are subject to disease challenges similar to those affecting other Poultry. The most important ones are listed and a brief description given below

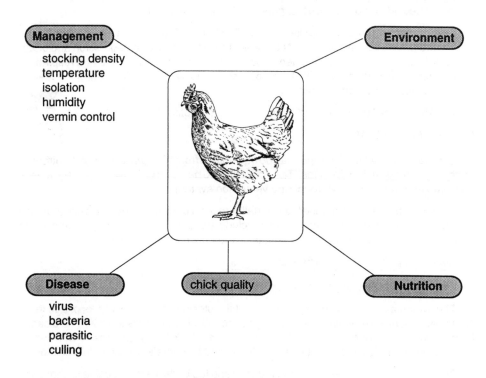

Management
- stocking density
- temperature
- isolation
- humidity
- vermin control

Environment

Disease
- virus
- bacteria
- parasitic
- culling

chick quality

Nutrition

The main diseases are as follows:

Newcastle Disease
Infectious Bronchitis
Infectious Bursal disease
Escherichia coli (E coli)
Salmonella
Coccidiosis
Broiler Ascitic Syndrome (Ascites)

Newcastle Disease (ND)

This disease is caused by a virus and is a **notifiable** disease. It is highly contagious through infected droppings and respiratory discharge between birds. Spread between farms by infected equipment, trucks, personnel, wild birds or air.

T he incubation period is usually between 3 to 6 days. Most commonly chickens and turkeys are affected by the disease. N.D. causes high mortality with depression and death in 3 to 5 days as major signs. Affected birds do not always show nervous and respiratory signs. There is no treatment for N.D. The only control is by vaccination during the rearing period (see vaccination programme).

The Ministry of Agriculture and the police must be notified.

Infectious Bronchitis (IB)

This is a viral infection. The virus can be transmitted from bird to bird through an airborne route, e.g. carried on dust particles. The virus can also be airborne between poultry houses and even from farm to farm through the ventilation system.

In younger birds I.B. can cause high mortality. In older birds I.B. does not cause mortality but does cause respiratory signs which include gurgling and wheezing. There is no treatment for I.B., prevention by vaccination is the best method of control.

Infectious Bursal Disease (GUMBORO)

This disease is causing serious losses in the UK

The symptoms vary according to the age of the stock. Less than 3 weeks of age there is very little mortality, but over 3 weeks of age mortality is from 10% to 25%. The disease lasts about 5 days during which time birds die, the flock looks depressed with ruffled feathers and there is increased thirst and depressed food intake resulting in wet litter.

The performance of the survivors is reduced and the birds are susceptible to challenge from other diseases, as IBD damages the Immuno Suppressive system.

Coccidiosis

This is a disease affecting the gut of the growing chicken caused by a protozoal parasite. There are 8 types, 6 of which can cause problems to broiler chickens. Symptoms include; huddling, depression, reduced food intake, blood stained droppings and mortality.

The disease is unlikely to occur because anti coccidial drugs are included in the ration. If it does, swift action is required as high mortality can result.

HEALTH

E. Coli

This is a bacteria. It causes secondary infections whilst or after the bird is suffering from something else. They often occur during a challenge of IB, and left untreated can lead to high % of downgrading from Coli Septicaemia in the broilers.

Poor hygiene can lead to high levels of E Coli which enter the bird orally giving similar results. It can be treated with antibiotics obtained on veterinary prescription.

Salmonella

Birds affected may show no symptoms. Most companies test for salmonella during the growing cycle. Positive tests are notifiable. Birds that appear unhealthy are stunted, crippled or injured should be removed from the flock, killed and incinerated.

Broiler Ascitic Syndrome (Ascities)

Birds abdomen fills with fluid. It is caused by a build up of the by products of metabolism. It is also associated with poor ventilation and oxygen supply. Mortality is low but many culls are evident, their bodies full of liquid and the skin reddish in colour. **There is no cure.**

Affected birds should be culled and attention given to ventilation, especially during the brooding period when gas fired brooders are being used.

Culling

The main reasons for culling birds out of a flock are problems associated with the legs. They appear to be caused by either:

> **very fast growth**
> **nutrition, or**
> **a combination of both**

To minimise these losses a reputable brand of broiler feed should be fed and alternative feed programmes should be used when superchicken or roaster production is considered.

Other Mortality

In any population there will be mortality. The accepted norm for 6 week broiler production would be 4-5% made up as follows:

Age	%	Reason
Day 1 to 10	1 to 1 $\frac{1}{2}$	Poor quality chicks delivered. Non starters - chicks not finding food, water, heat etc.
Day 10 to 14 14-21 21-28 28-35	$\frac{1}{2}$ $\frac{1}{2}$ $\frac{1}{2}$ $\frac{1}{2}$	May be some organ failure especially liver & kidney. Nonspecific - chicks having survived weakening
35-42	1	Heart attacks

Management

In order to maintain health the following points should be observed.

Stocking density	Broilers should be stocked at a maximum of 34 kg/m² in controlled environment housing. This figure may only be reached in the final few days of growing. During the hot summer months it may be advisable to reduce the stocking either:- by placing less initially or by thinning at around 35 days to prevent heavy losses due to the heat stress.
Overstocking	Leads to increased competition, poorer performance, bad litter etc. Unfortunately it is often practiced because it reduces overheads.
Understocking	Wastage of resources. Costs spread over few birds
Isolation	The site should be isolated from other poultry stocks and from unwanted visitors to prevent the introduction of disease. Vehicles should be washed before entry to the farm.
Cleanout	The site should be totally depopulated, cleaned out, washed down and disinfected between crops to prevent the carryover of disease from one crop to the next. The practice of total depopulation and then restocking is known as ALL IN ALL OUT.
Vermin Control	Vermin should be discouraged by good housekeeping measures, such as; secure storage of food; hygienic disposal of dead birds; regular baiting for rats and mice.
Environment	It is important that the environment is maintained in a broiler house to ensure the birds reach their potential.
Temperature	High, low or fluctuating temperatures are undesirable, young chicks being the most susceptible. Low humidities lead to poor feathering, and dusty conditions which can cause respiratory problems.

Humidity	High humidities can cause poor litter and the problems associated with it. High humidities together with high temperatures can lead to heat stress as the bird cannot cool itself.
Ventilation	Adequate supply of fresh air is essential to provide the birds with oxygen and cooling. Inadequate ventilation can be the predisposing factor to Broiler Ascitic Syndrome. Environment must be monitored and alarmed for High/Low temperature and power failure.
Nutritional	There should be few problems associated with nutrition so long as reputable feeds are used. Problems may occur when old food is used that has become contaminated by moulds or fungi and the vitamin content has diminished.
Stress	Whatever the cause anything that upsets the bird will put it under pressure or "stress" leaving it vulnerable to attack from other enemies such as virus, bacteria etc.

DISEASE PREVENTION

Disease is prevented by a number of measures

> **General hygiene precautions**
> **Good management**
> **Correct environment**
> **Nutrition**

In addition to the above, vaccination should be employed to give birds protection against the important virus diseases that present a threat.

Vaccination of broilers differs according to

1 The risk of infection

If disease is in the locality then the birds must be adequately vaccinated.

2 The state of immunity of the broiler parents

All broiler parents undergo a comprehensive programme of vaccination in order to give themselves protection and so that they can pass this protection on to their offspring through the egg. This protection is called MATERNAL IMMUNITY and it is this that is relied upon to protect the broiler throughout its life.

When the broiler parents start to age, this immunity and therefore the immunity passed on starts to wane. Chicks hatched from these eggs need vaccinating.

HEALTH

An example of a vaccination programme is given below, however it will be modified as the disease situation changes and on veterinary advice.

Age	Disease	Vaccination	
Day Old (Hatching)	IB	H 120 (Spray)	
14 days	Gumboro (IBD) IB Newcastle Disease	Bursine 2 (Water) IB H 120 Water HBI Water	} Combined
21 days	Gumboro	Bursine 2 (Water)	

IB = Infectious Bronchitis. Vaccine called H120
IBD = Infectious Bursal Disease = Gumboro. Vaccine called Bursine 2.

Other vaccines can be incorporated, for example Newcastle Disease could be added to the IB at 14 days. Veterinary advice should be sought when considering vaccination programmes. Where Newcastle Disease vaccine is used it is known as Hitchner B1.

Coccidiosis

At the present time coccidiosis is controlled by medication in the feed. Vaccines are just becoming available but cost are prohibitive for this class of stock.

Vaccination Efficiency

This should be monitored by blood tests 2-3 weeks after vaccinating to assess the protection the birds have. Should it be low or disease occurs, then the following should be considered.

> **Does the programme need modifying?**
> **Are vaccines being administered correctly?**
> **Are the vaccines covering the strains of disease being encountered?**

When using vaccines check storage requirements, expiry dates etc and record the procedure and information for future reference.

Housing includes the following elements:

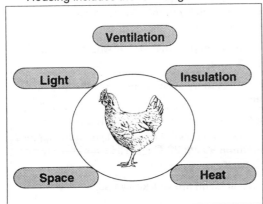

Ventilation

Ventilation requirements vary according to age, size, feed consumption, house temperature etc. Good ventilation supplies:

Oxygen
Cool air

and removes:

Carbon Dioxide
Water vapour
Dust
Ammonia

Should ventilation be inadequate the birds will suffer, resulting in depressed growth rates, or if it is due to high temperatures, heat stress and mortality.

KEY FACTS

A formula can be used to calculate the ventilaton requirements of broilers based on the amount of food eaten.

> **Maximum requirement 20 m³of air/second for every tonne of food eaten/day**
>
> **Maximum requirement 2 m³ of air/second for every tonne of food eaten/day**

e.g. 10,000 broilers eating 130 grams of food/day = 1,300 kg or 1.3 tonnes
Ventilation requirement = 20 x 1.3 = 26m²/second

A 610mm fan gives 2.6m³/second, therefore 10 fans are required. For minimum ventilation, e.g. overnight to keep the air clear but not remove heat, the requirement is 1/10, so only one fan would be used.

As a rule of thumb one 610mm fan is required for every 1,000 broilers housed. Fans are operated automatically by thermostats with an override function to service minimum ventilation requirements as necessary.

Outsiders Guide

HOUSING

Ventilation controls the following:

Ammonia	Can be smelled at 20 ppm or above. Too high a concentration of ammonia is dangerous: 10 ppm will damage surface of lungs 20 ppm will increase susceptibility to respiratory viruses 50 ppm will reduce growth rate By law, there is a legal maximum permitted level which is 25 ppm for an 8 hour shift (Factory Act).
Dust	Dust will damage the respiratory system and leave the bird more susceptible to disease.
Humidity	High humidities lead to poor litter and increased downgrading. In addition the bird's ability to cool itself is reduced as relative humidity (RH) rises. Temperatures above 29°C and RH over 70% cause severe growth depression.
Insulation	The benefits of good insulation are well known as: retaining heat in in winter maintaining cool conditions in summer preventing condensation Bad insulation means that you will have high heating bills and bad litter and high downgrading.
Heat	Chicks require supplementary heat for the first few weeks of life. There are several programmes for brooding, two of which are given below.
Method 1	

Temp in °C

Brooder Temperature initially 35°C

House Temperature

21°C post brooding

Age in days

The brooder temperature is reduced by 2°C to 3°C per week on a daily basis. Ventilation is increased as required. As the brooder temperature drops so does the house temperature. The brooders are not used much from 3 weeks onwards as most of the heat comes from the body heat of the birds.

Once the birds have been weaned off heat at about 30 days (depending on the time of year) a house temperature of 21°C should be maintained - this is known as the **post brooding temperature**.

Method 2

House temperature °C	Age in days	House temperature °C	Age in days
32	1	30	2
29	3	28	4
27	5	27	6
26	7	26	8
25	9	25	10
24	11	24	12
23	13	23	14
22	14	22	16
21	17	21	18 to kill

Each programme has its advantages and disadvantages.

Heat is provided by brooders powered by gas or electricity, they can provide spot heating or heat the whole house.

Post brooding temperature

21°C is adopted as the PBT as it gives the best results. If the temperature is higher - food consumption and growth rate are reduced. If the temperature is lower - higher food consumption but not proportionately more growth.

Stocking Density

The area of floor space per broiler is dependent upon:

> **Processing age**
> **Climate and season**
> **Type of housing**

In the UK, the Ministry Welfare Code recommends stocking densities at differing liveweights to obtain a biomass of 34.22 kg/m² and these are given on the next page.

HOUSING

Liveweight kg	Birds/m²	Liveweight/kg	Birds/m²
1.0	34.2	2.4	14.3
1.2	28.5	2.6	13.2
1.4	24.4	2.8	12.2
1.6	21.4	3.0	11.4
1.8	19.0	3.2	10.7
2.0	17.1	3.4	10.0
2.2	15.6	3.6	9.5

Source: Ros Breeders

Notes:

The recommendation is 34kg/m². Many people stock in excess of these figures. In hot weather with birds in the last week of life many suffer from heat stress and die. Pressure is on to reduce stocking densities to possibly 28 kg/m² for the summer months. Reducing stocking by 20% will increase overheads accordingly, putting those producers that comply with legislation at a disadvantage.

Floor Litter

Broilers are grown on litter on the floor. Cage rearing and rearing on slats or wire floors have been tried but have not been successful. There are a choice of litters available.

FLOOR LITTER	NOTES
White wood shavings	Traditionally the most popular but now rather expensive. Amount required = 0.5 tonnes/100m².
Chopped straw	Becoming very popular, should be chopped into 25mm lengths and preferably treated with a fungicide. Growth rates on chopped straw appear to be slightly poorer than those on white wood shavings. Amount required 0.5 tonnes/100m².
Shredded newspaper	Expensive to buy but very small amounts required. Does not seem to work as well as the first two products. Amount required 0.1 tonnes/100m².
"Litterite"	Milled and pelleted straw product - highly absorbent giving good results. Expensive but small amounts required. Relatively dust free and easy to spread. Amount required 0.25 to 0.3 tonnes/100m².
	Straw based litters will probably become more popular in the future. Farms with an arable enterprise could use straw which may otherwise be a nuisance, treating it with a fungicide as it is chopped. Other products are becoming available for adding to the straw. One example would be a chemical that reduces the ammonia in the litter..

HOUSING

Lighting

Several lighting patterns are employed

Age in days	Intensity	Day length in hours
0-7	20 lux	23 light 1 dark
7-21	20 gradually reduced to 3 lux	23 light 1 dark
21 - kill	1-3 lux	23 light 1 dark
Intermittent Light Programme		
Age in days	Intensity	Day length in hours
0-7	20 lux	23 light 1 dark
7-21	20 gradually reduced to 3 lux	23 light 1 dark
21 - kill	1-3 lux	2 hours light 2 hours dark

The intermittent programme may improve efficiency and product quality.

Light Intensity

Low light intensity gives better performance but welfare organisations are concerned about the rearing of livestock in continuous dim light conditions. Some producers are now rearing on bright light all the way through only dimming if vice occurs.

KEY FACTS - HOUSING

Stocking density	34 kg/m² Approx 17.5 days 'as hatched' birds/m² @ 42 days
Ventilation needs	1 x 610 mm fan/1000 42 day old broilers (max.)
Temperature	Gradually reduced over 17-30 days to 21°C
Light	23 hours light/day. Intensity reduced gradually from bright to dim
Feeder space	45 broilers (to 6 weeks old) per 1m of chain/rack 15 pans/1000 broilers (to 6 weeks old)
Drinkers	8-10 bell drinkers/1000 22 birds/nipple

REPRODUCTION

INTRODUCTION

Broiler production is a purely rearing enterprise. Broiler units are not involved in the reproduction of breeding stock. This aspect is left entirely to the hatcheries, and the broiler breeding companies.

REARING OF BROILER CHICKS

The rearing of broilers can be described under the following headings:

> **Food**
> **Water**
> **Light**
> **Temperature/ventilation**

Food

Broiler starter crumbs are placed in the automatic feeders and in the supplementary feeders (these may be trays or lengths of corrugated cardboard etc.). The feed is replenished as it gets eaten. Chicks must find food soon after they are placed in the house.

The supplementary feeders are removed after 7 days. Automatic feeders provided.

NB Automatic feeders should be set to come on more often as the birds grow to ensure feed is available all the time as the appetite increases.

Water

Water is placed in the automatic founts and in the supplementaries just before the chicks arrive.

Plenty of drinker points are needed to ensure the chicks find water within the first few hours of housing. The supplementary drinkers are removed gradually from around 6 days and the automatic founts are raised as the chicks grow. Clean water is essential, bell type drinkers will need cleaning initially daily, latterly less often. **NB** Water is provided ad lib.

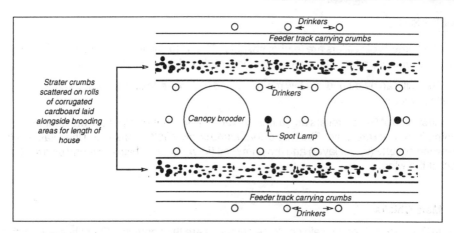

Strater crumbs scattered on rolls of corrugated cardboard laid alongside brooding areas for length of house

Drinkers

Feeder track carrying crumbs

Drinkers

Canopy brooder

Spot Lamp

Feeder track carrying crumbs

Drinkers

Light

The timelock controlling the lights should be set to give 23 hours light 1 hour dark.

The right intensity is bright (20 lux+) for the first week to enable the chicks to find food, water etc. Spot lights are sometimes employed and suspended near to the brooders to keep chicks near to the heat. Light intensity may be reduced after the first week if so desired or if vice problems occur.

Temperature/Ventilation

The brooders are lit 24 hours before the chicks arrive to ensure the house is heated thoroughly. The temperature is reduced on a daily basis in accordance with the programme. Brooders can be removed when no longer in use.

Ventilation is provided from day 1. As the demand for ventilation increases the vents are opened wider and the fans are switched, on being controlled automatically using thermostats.

REPRODUCTION

Feather Sexing

Most breeds of broilers are feather sexable. That is to say their sex can be determined from the feather pattern of the wings on the first day of life.

The skill can be gained in a few moments and high speeds and accuracy achieved with a little practice.

All strains of Ross Broilers are feather sexable. Fast feathering chicks are female, slow feathering chicks are male. The type of feathering is identified by observing the relationship between coverts (upper layer) and the primaries (lower layer) which are found on the outer half of the wing.

Male Chicks

In the slow feathering male chick the primaries are the same length or shorter than the coverts

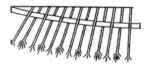

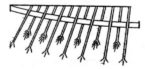

Female Chicks

In the fast feathering female chick the primaries are longer than the coverts.

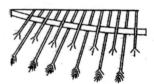

PERFORMANCE

PHYSICAL PERFORMANCE

The following figures are actual performance and costings from across the country. They are averages and it should be remembered that there will be figures that are better and worse than those printed.

KEY ASSESSMENT QUESTIONS

Turnround	65.8 days
Killing Age	46 days
Stocking Density	41.3 kgs/m²
At Killing Age	2.242kgs
Mortality	6.5%
FCR	2.03

GROSS MARGINS

OUTPUT PER BIRD		p
Sale	2.3kg (6-7 weeks) @ 59.5p/kg	136.85
Less	chick cost	21
	chick mortality 6.5%	1.4
TOTAL		**114.45**
Variable Costs		
	Concentrates 4.6kg @ 18.5p/kg	85.1
	Heat & electricity	4
	Litter	3
	Variable sundries (Vet, med, ins)	4.7
TOTAL		**96.8**

Source: ABC1994

PERFORMANCE

Although all the figures here are given in kgs, many packers and growers still prefer to work in imperial units.

Production figures for Free Range, Additive free and Corn Fed broilers are difficult to obtain.

They would no doubt be much more lucrative, however the market is limited.

Before embarking on broiler production it is vital to obtain a contract with a processor. Never place broiler chicks hoping to find an outlet for them during the six week growing period.

Industry Outlook

The chicken industry has benefited from continued growth over the last 10 years. Over this period output has risen 42% while turkey has managed 33%.

Imports show a decline of 14% for 1993 on the previous year to 149000 tonnes according to M.A.F.F. What is certain there was a fall in imports last year but the figure may be inaccurate due to change in the way the data is collected within the EU.

EU production continues to grow - total poultrymeat output increased by 84,000 tonnes in 1993. In addition to this production in other countries dwarfs the U.K. production - one U.S. company (Tyson) produces 2.6 times the total U.K. production of broilers - with cheaper feed and in some cases labour this enables chicken from non EU countries to arrive here cheaper than our own production costs. Marketing will become even more important in the next few years.

PERFORMANCE

USEFUL FORMULAE

Formulae for calculating performance

FCR   <u>**Food eaten in kgs**</u>   fig should be approx 1.8
        total liveweight sold kgs

FCR can be misleading. Low figures can be obtained meaning food saved but other costs may increase in doing so.

EPEF = European Performance Efficiency Factor   figure for 1992 should be 230 or
                                                      more

<u>**Liveability x Liveweight in kg**</u> **x 100**
age in days x FCR

eg   AH Flock 42 days weight 1940
          Mortality 4.9% FCR 1.83

         EPEF =   <u>**95.1 x 1.94**</u>   **x 100 = 240**
                          42 x 1.83

The higher the figure the better. It is used extensively in EC to compare farms within a company or country but cannot be used to compare performances between countries.

A FCR gives a figure for converting feed. This can be influenced by house temperatures etc. The EPEF however takes into account other factors and some people prefer to use it believing it gives a better picture of efficiency. The figure is constantly increasing. A good EPEF for 1993 would be around 250 the current record being 270.

The most accurate measure of efficiency when comparing enterprises or farms is profit/ unit area.

PERFORMANCE

THE
OUTSIDER'S GUIDE
to
DAIRY

1995 Edition

THE
OUTSIDER'S GUIDE
to
DAIRY

1995 Edition

PRODUCTION

INTRODUCTION

The UK dairy industry was for many years the backbone of livestock farming. With a secure market the industry thrived from 1944 to 1984, and herd sizes increased from 20 cows to almost 100.

Due to similar expansion across Europe, the EU decided that the cost of maintaining an ever increasing reserve mountain of butter and skim milk powder was too high. A farm quota scheme was introduced in 1984. Since then, the number of dairy cows and dairy farmers has fallen. Having shed the surplus production by 1989, the industry has stabilised and provides a respectable living for the remaining dairy farmers.

EUROPEAN PRODUCTION

Milk Production In The EU ('000000 tonnes)

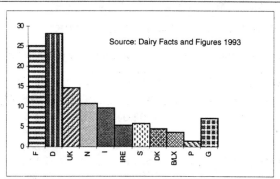

Source: Dairy Facts and Figures 1993

Average Number Of Cows Per Herd

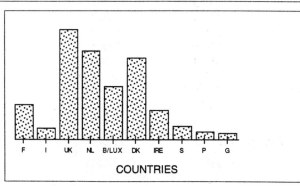

COUNTRIES

Source: E.E.C. Dairy Facts and Figures, 1992.

Dairying and management systems differ widely between countries. Although the UK lies third in total milk production and number of cows within the EU, herd size is the largest in Europe. Most other countries have large numbers of small herds.

PRODUCTION

THE UK

Milk yield per cow is one measure of output efficiency.

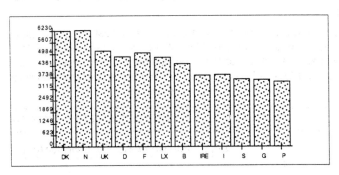

Annual Yield (kg/cow)

Source: E.E.C. Dairy Facts
and Figures, 1992.

Number of Producers And Herd Sizes In Various Regions Of UK

The UK is divided into 5 regions, each with a share of the national quota.

Region	Million litres	No. of producers
Northern	1208.0	3,432
North West	2563.6	6,944
East	286.7	584
East Midlands	524.2	1,146
West Midlands	1185.4	2,807
North Wales	470.2	1,672
South Wales	859.8	3,192
Southern	493.4	896
Mid West	1655.3	3,236
Far West	1397.0	3,961
South East	467.4	859
Scottish M.M.B. Region	996.5	2178
Aberdeen and District	104.9	165
North of Scotland	56.1	95
Northern Ireland	1170.5	6,379
TOTAL ENGLAND &WALES	**11111.1**	**28,729**
TOTAL UK	**13439**	**37,217**

Source: Dairy Facts and Figures, 1993.

PRODUCTION

PRODUCTION SEASONALITY

i Traditionally, calving takes place during the autumn and winter, with most milk produced from stored winter feeds.

ii Milk yields rise to a peak by about week 5 (35 - 50 days after calving), the peak persists for 3-4 weeks.

iii The cow has 6 weeks for a dry, rest period between annual calvings.

Half of a cow's total yield is produced in the first 100 days, giving maximum supply to the winter milk market. This is followed by a spring peak when cows are turned out to graze in April and May, and then a milk drought in the late summer.

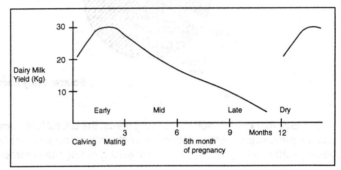

Milk Consumption

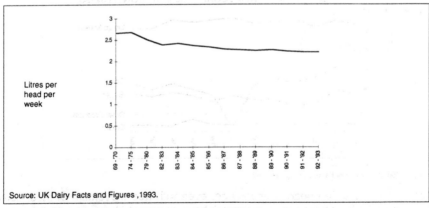

Source: UK Dairy Facts and Figures ,1993.

Raw milk is a food and a material for processing to other foods.

Approximately half the annual production is consumed as liquid milk (208 pints or 118 litres/person/year; weekly average 4 pt or 2.23 litres), taking priority over processing to butter, cheese, cream etc. Because production is seasonal, manufacturers have to cope with a fluctuating supply which causes problems.

OUTSIDER'S GUIDE

UK Utilisation Of Milk

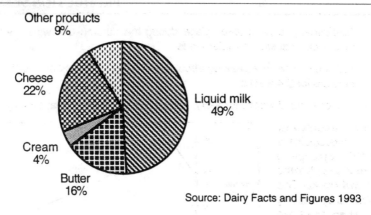

Source: Dairy Facts and Figures 1993

Due to predominantly autumn-calving herds, the UK suffers from a significant seasonal fluctuation in milk production. With quota restraints, manufacturers (especially of butter and cheese) suffer shortages of milk for processing during the summer.

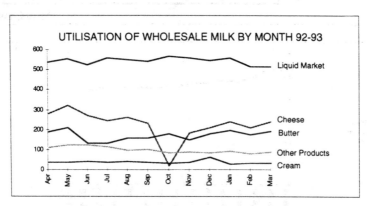

Source: UK Dairy Facts and Figures 1993

Because this is a European phenomenon, even with free movement of most dairy products within the EU, cheese and butter prices have increased. However, with free trade across Europe (from 1993), forecasts for growing demands for cheese could lead to greater imports of raw milk for processing.

To encourage a more uniform milk supply by increasing spring-calving, Milk Marque pay higher prices (seasonality bonus) for milk produced in the months of July to October. (See 🗂)

OUTSIDER'S GUIDE

KEY ASSESSMENT QUESTIONS

Milk output/cow(litres)	5550
Milk composition % fat	>3.8
% protein	>3.3
Target calving interval (days)	365
Herd replacement rate (%)	22 - 25/year
Stocking rate cows/ha	1.9
Concentrates 0.27kg/l, 1.49t @£142/t (£)	213
Margin over concentrates (£)	1062
Margin over purchased feeds (£)	937
Gross margin / cow (£)	**856** (After deduction of **forage costs**)
Gross margin / ha (£)	**1797** (After deduction of **forage costs**)

FACTORS AFFECTING DAIRY PROFITABILITY

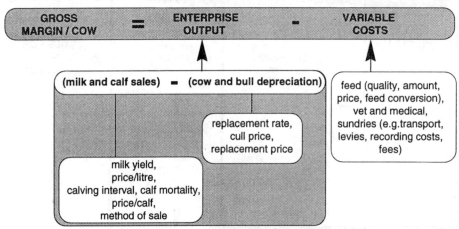

| GROSS MARGIN / COW | = | ENTERPRISE OUTPUT | − | VARIABLE COSTS |

(milk and calf sales) − (cow and bull depreciation)

replacement rate, cull price, replacement price

feed (quality, amount, price, feed conversion), vet and medical, sundries (e.g.transport, levies, recording costs, fees)

milk yield, price/litre, calving interval, calf mortality, price/calf, method of sale

Gross margin / hectare = (G.M. per cow x stocking rate/hectare)

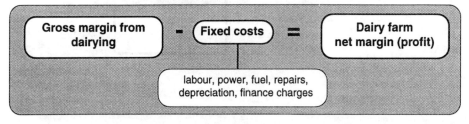

| Gross margin from dairying | − | Fixed costs | = | Dairy farm net margin (profit) |

labour, power, fuel, repairs, depreciation, finance charges

PRODUCTION

THE PRODUCTION CYCLE

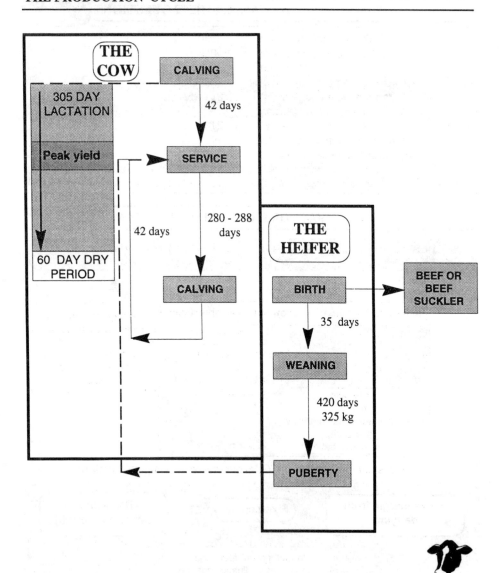

MARKETING

PRODUCTS

Liquid milk is the **primary product** and approximately 49% of milk in the UK is consumed as such.

Raw milk can be processed into a wide range of **secondary products** with differing fat content; cream, skimmed milk, butter, cheeses, yogurts and lactose. These allow the valuable nutrient constituents to be preserved.

MARKET OUTLETS

A producer owned Milk Marketing Board was set up in 1933, covering all milk produced in England and Wales. This was in response to the difficulties that producers had in negotiating prices with local dairies. Scotland joined in 1934 and Northern Ireland had similar arrangements soon after.

The Old Situation

Five Marketing Boards covered the UK; The Milk Marketing Board of England and Wales; The Aberdeen and District Board; The North of Scotland Board; The Scottish Board and The Northern Ireland Board. The country was also subdivided into regions.

Each Board was controlled by elected members representing dairy farmers, and appointed members from industry or government who were not answerable to politicians but were intended to add expertise to the Board.

The Boards had to, by law, buy and find a market for all the cows milk which was offered to them provided it complied with certain quality standards. Producers had to sell to or through the Board and the Board had to buy all milk which it is offered. These powers only relate to milk sold in liquid form.

Milk Marque

The Milk Marketing Scheme ended on the 1st November 1994. Farmers are now free to sell their milk direct to the dairy companies or continue to sell through a marketing organisation.

In anticipation of these changes the Milk Marketing Board for England and Wales has established a new Co-operative "Milk Marque". Over 70% of all dairy farmers joined the new co-operative who will collect and sell their milk. Technical services, National Milk Records and Genus breeding management and health care are now idependent companies.

Dairy Crest has also become an independent company, dairy farmers being issued with shares in the new company. Dairy Crest competes with the other companies e.g. Northern Foods, Avonmore and Nestlé to buy milk on the open market.

MARKETING

Quotas

The EU imposed a quota system in 1984 of a base quota of 1983 production less 9%, in an attempt to regain the balance between production and demand.

Quotas can be transferred or leased only within the old Milk Board Region. Leasing through the National Intervention Board allows quota transfer without lands transfer, however in all other situations quota transfer has to be accompanied by land transfer.

Services

There are a number of services available to dairy farmers:

- ☛ on farm milk recording for herd management (now N.M.R.)
- ☛ other farm management advice (Genus)
- ☛ silage and forage analysis and sale of a silage additive (Genus)
- ☛ analysis of milk samples for Brucellosis for M.A.F.F.
- ☛ pregnancy tests
- ☛ cell count/bacteriology of milk samples.

The Boards ran milk quality testing laboratories to which milk from all dairy farms and creameries is sent for quality assessment on a routine basis. At the time of writing there is uncertainty over who will be owning/ running what service. (23 - 11 - 94)

MARKET REQUIREMENTS

i   Individual producers have to be registered with M.A.F.F. and have to have a milk quota.

ii Having obtained government authority, the farmer registers with the appropriate regional authority.

iii The farmer then requires a contract with a processor or a licence to sell direct to consumers.

Most producers are wholesalers and are allowed to sell direct to the processors like Milk Marque, who arrange collection of their milk daily.   Provided the milk reaches minimum standards of composition and hygienic quality the producer has no other marketing worries for these are taken care of by the processors.

Pricing

The price paid to the farmer for milk is calculated on the % of protein and fat in each month's supply. There must be no antibiotic residues, extra water or other contaminants, and stringent tests are carried out to detect bacterial spoilage which can result from poor milking hygiene. Bulk milk cell counts also effect price per litre.

MARKETING

MILK HYGIENE QUALITY

Taints
bad smells, colour of milk resulting from contamination or disease, seen before removal from the farm.

Antibiotic residues
resulting from contamination by antibiotics used to treat cows.

Freezing point
accidental contamination with washing water changes milk freeezing point and can be easily detected.

Sediment
poor washing of udders or teats can allow minute particles of soil, straw, etc. to pass through older types of milk filters.

Total bacterial count
Coliform and other bacteria contaminate milk particularly if machinery is poorly washed or sterilised between milkings. They may also come from heavily infected cows.

(T.B.C. colonies/ml)	
Band A	<20,000
Band B	21,000 - 100,000
Band C	>100,000

Milk is sampled weekly from the farm bulk tank, and the samples are tested in central testing laboratories. Individual dairies may also do their own tests.

Licenced producer-retailers sell direct to shops or doorstep rather than to the Board. Unless exempt, the milk must be pasteurized. This can be done on the farm using small scale equipment, or at a local dairy by special arrangement. In 1993, a total of 1,326 producer-retailers were registered in the UK compared to 11,255 in 1965. This was out of a total of 37,217 registered producers in 1994 and 124,688 in 1965. (Source: M.M.B. Dairy Facts & Figures, 1993.)

MILK PRICING

Key Points

i   Price is decided by composition.
ii   National price relates to average value of milk sold.
iii Monthly adjustments are made for hygienic quality.

1994 values:

At 1st Sept 1994	Fat	Protein
pence per 1%	2.292	3.580

MARKETING

If composition was:	Fat	4.10%
	Protein	3.29%
Producer price:	Fat	4.10 x 2.292 = 9.3972p/litre
	Protein	3.29 x 3.580 = 11.7782p/litre
Basic price per litre:		**21.11754p**

After the basic price is calculated, **seasonal** adjustments are made.

Month:	Price change	Month:	Price change
April '94	-10%	October	+5.0%
May	-12.5		
June	-5		
July	+15		
August	+15		
September	+10		

Total bacterial count band adjustments are made:

Band A	0.0 p/litre
Band B	-0.25 p/litre
Band C	-2.0 p/litre

If milk was band **C** during the previous 6 months, deduct 6.0p/litre. If 6.0p has been deducted in previous 6 months, deduct 10.0p/litre.

Confirmed failure of antibiotics test: producer is paid 1.00 p/litre only. He receives a warning and advisory visits to help overcome the hygiene problem.

Bulk Milk Cell Count Payments

A system of bonus payments and deductions is also applied to the standard milk price based on the somatic cell count of the milk. Farmers have been notified of their somatic cell counts on each milk cheque since October 1990, and the payments scheme will be based on a three month rolling average of the reported counts. The bonus and levy payments will be as follows:

< 400,000 cells	Band 1	nil
401-500,000 cells	Band 2	-0.5p/l
501,000-1,000,000	Band 3	-1.0p/l
> 1,000,000	Band 4	-2.0p/l

BREEDS & SYSTEMS

INTRODUCTION

The **system** relates to the season of the year when cows calve, the **breed** determines the genetic limits within which management must optimise production.

MAIN BREEDS

The majority of UK dairy cows are of black and white Friesian or Holstein makeup. Other breeds include: Jersey, Guernsey, Dairy Shorthorn and Ayrshire.

Holstein bloodlines, imported in the 1960's, have been used to increase lactation yield and cow size in many originally British Friesian herds. The commercial Friesian cow is more often than not a mixture of British Friesian and Holstein.

Percentage Of Cows In Each Dairy Breed In The UK

	Eng & Wales	Scotland	N. Ireland
Holstein	3.4	4.1	-
British Friesan	74.5	61.4	98.1
Ayrshire	1.9	12.6	1.2
Shorthorn	0.4	-	0.4
Guernsey	1.4	} 0.5	-
Jersey	1.7		-
Fr x H	16.2	11.1	-
Fr x Ayr	-	10.3	-
Others	0.3	0.1	0.3

Source: Dairy Facts and Figures, 1993

Joint registration in the Friesian and Holstein pedigree herd books has made it increasingly difficult to differentiate between Holstein and Friesian cattle. The common approach is to call all black and white dairy cows Friesian-Holsteins.

Holstein genetic content of young bulls under test by Genus.

	1973-74	1987-88
Bulls with Holstein blood	9%	92.3%
Average Holstein genetic content	5.2%	62.6%

BREEDS & SYSTEMS

TYPICAL PERFORMANCE OF DAIRY COWS IN THE UK

Breed	Typical milk yield		Analysis		
	Yield range (kgs)	fat %	protein %	mature weight (kgs)	
N. American/ Dutch Holstein	6483 - 6703	3.82 - 3.91	3.14 - 3.18	650	
British Friesian	5800 - 5925	3.86 - 3.94	3.20 - 3.24	585	
Ayrshire	5260 - 5352	3.92 - 3.98	3.29 - 3.33	500	
Dairy Shorthorn	5175 - 5195	3.63 - 3.75	3.26 - 3.28	485	
Guernsey	4275 - 4285	4.66 - 4.74	3.54 - 3.58	485	
Jersey	4047 - 4163	5.31 - 5.39	3.80 - 3.84	385	
Dexter	2308 - 2362	4.0 - 4.16	3.45 - 3.47	300	

Liquid milk is sold to the processors. Payment is based upon total weight of fat, protein and lactose, hence the popularity of the high yielding Holstein.

The Jersey and Guernsey with higher milk solids, are kept to provide the Channel Island Milk market. This milk receives a premium because of its high fat level.

CLASSIFICATION

The breeds show clear differences in body shape (conformation) and various schemes have been devised to classify cows:

e.g. **linear scoring**:

15 different body areas are assessed, scores (1 to 9, with 5 the mid point) describe where the particular cow fits within the breed range for each character.

Temperament and ease of milking are also scored in the Friesian breed (giving 17 scores).

Linear score techniques allow comparisons between breeds. The Genus organisation uses a "Breeding Value" based on a combination of linear score and yield potential.

SYSTEMS OF PRODUCTION

Breed of stock has little effect on the overall system of production. The time of year when maximum milk is expected to be sold determines the production system centred around the different calving dates required. Dairy farms are split into systems by the calving season.

Calving Seasons For Various Systems

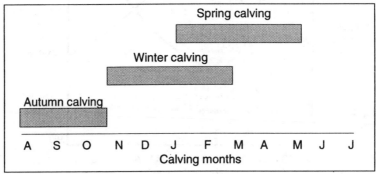

The calving season affects when cows have their highest needs for nutrients, determining whether they use winter forages or summer grazing to gain most milk.

Spring Calving

Cows need little high quality winter feed. The critical first third of the lactation is spent feeding on high quality and nutritious spring grass. The later stages of lactation (autumn and early winter) can be supported by poorer quality roughages. This system is inappropriate in low rainfall areas where mid season grass growth is slow.

Autumn Calving

Cows will spend the critical first third of their lactation on conserved forages (silage, purchased feeds and home mixed concentrates). The enterprise management must be aimed towards poorer summer grazing and high quality grassland conservation.

Autumn calvers usually out yield spring calvers due to the boost in yield when turned out to grass in the spring.

Other Considerations

Quotas are met by high yields from a few cows or lower yields from a greater number of cows. This depends on the amount and quality of grass, amount of land available and the quota size. Also to be considered is the interaction of dairying with other enterprises on mixed farms and price incentives from the M.M.B'.s to encourage summer calving.

BREEDS & SYSTEMS

Proportions Of Milk From Grass/Forage And From Concentrate

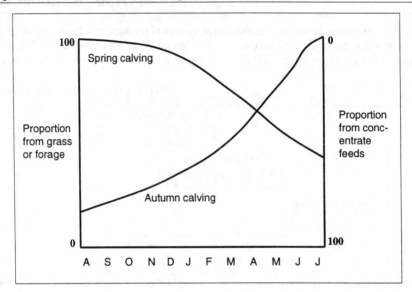

Spring calving

Proportion from grass or forage

Proportion from concentrate feeds

Autumn calving

A S O N D J F M A M J J

NUTRITION

FEEDING AIMS

These are to optimise **milk yield** and **quality** from the dairy cow and to produce **a calf a year** .

DIET

The dairy cow's diet is made up of a mixture of dry roughages, high water content succulents, manufactured compound concentrates and straights (high energy or protein by-products of industrial processing). A typical ration might contain 60 to 80% of conserved forage or grazed grass and 20 to 40% of compound or straight concentrates.

Succulents	normally eaten fresh except silages which are "pickled" by fermentation to enable storage e.g. grass, cabbage, kale, grass silage, other silages. Low in dry-matter, usually >70% moisture content.
Dry forages	usually winter feed or used when grazing is in short supply e.g. hay, barley, straw, oat straw, straws treated with ammonium hydroxide or sodium hydroxide.
Straights	used to supplement home grown forages e.g. sugar beet pulp, brewers grains, soyabean meal, palm kernel cake, maize gluten meal.
Concentrates	compound feeds bought in to supplement home produced or straight feeds.

FEED TARGETS

Cows are fed for: i   production which includes milk and calves

ii   bodyweight maintenance and change

iii   growth

Rations are commonly calculated using metabolisable energy, metabolisable protein and digestible crude protein (D.C.P.) requirements, normally on a feed dry matter basis. More sophisticated systems involving an element of computer modelling and cost analysis can provide more precise or economically favourable answers.

OUTSIDER'S GUIDE

NUTRITION

Standards used: (daily requirements for 600 kg cow)

Maintenance   63 M.J. of M.E. and 345 grammes of D.C.P.
If the cow is in calf 86 M.J. are required for the last 100 days of pregnancy

Growth   34 M.J. per kg of weight increase

Milk yield   5.4 M.J. per kg of milk of average compositional quality
63g D.C.P. per kg of milk produced

Nutrient intake depends upon the cow's appetite which varies through lactation, being lowest after calving. The cows appetite may be generally calculated from:

Dry matter intake (kg/day) = (0.025 X bodyweight +(0.1X milk yield kg)

Therefore, a 600 kg Friesian with af milk yield of 20 kg, the standard appetite will be 17kgs of dry matter, or at 30 kgs yield it will be18 kgs.

Example

Calculation for a 600 kg cow:

Requirements.	D.M. kg	M.E. M.J./kg D.M.	D.C.P. g/kg D.M.
Dry matter intake	17	-	-
Maintenance 600kg	-	63	345
Pregnancy	-	23	-
Liveweight gain 0.5 kg/day	-	17	-
Production 20kgs @ 5MJ/kg		100	1000
Total	**17**	**203**	**1345**

To be supplied from a mixed ration.

Example of concentrate and forage analysis: Silage analysis is particularly variable with seasonal weather, grass growth and maturity, and quality of the ensilage process.

	D.M. %	M.E. M.J./kg D.M.	D.C.P. g/kg D.M.
Grass silage (good)	26	11.0	115
Grass silage (average)	24	10.5	80
Brewers grains	22	10.4	155
Sugar beet pulp	90	12.3	60
Soya meal	90	12.3	445
Typical dairy concentrate	86	13.0	140

The cow's needs would be met by:

Provides... / Diet component	Fresh weight kg	D.M. kg	M.E. (M.J.)	D.C.P. (g)
Good silage	35	9	91	1035
Purchased concentrate	6	5.2	68	725
Sugar beet pulp	2	1.8	22	108
Barley straw (sodium hydroxide treated)	1	1	7	0
Total offered		**17**	**196**	**1871**

% forage in D.M. = 59%

FEEDING PLANS

Flat rate - cows are fed one level of concentrate supplement to forage throughout their lactation. High milking cows are expected to be more efficient in food utilisation than low yielders, and have a larger appetite.

Stepped feeding - level of concentrate supplement is high early in lactation, then reduced by 2 or 3 stepped amounts as yield declines. The advantage over flat rate feeding is that the cows are not overfed at the end of lactation, nor underfed in early lactation. Forage is used to an increasing proportion as yield falls off.

Complete diet - the fully mixed diet is offered to cows with 24 hour access so they can eat to appetite. High yield cows are assumed to eat more than low yielders or be more efficient at converting to milk.

Incomplete-complete feed - a basic mixed diet is offered to cows. This provides a maintenance ration plus a basic level for milk yield. High yielders are then topped up, either by an extra feed of concentrate or straights in troughs or during milking from parlour feeders.

Lead feeding - cows are offered concentrate feeds in advance of anticipated yield to boost yields to genetic potential. Normally done in the first 80 to 100 days of lactation until peak yield is reached. The extra concentrate is recouped from reduced feeding in the last third of lactation.

Self feed system - cows are given free access to the silage clamp, held off by an electric wire or rail or tombstone barrier which is moved forward a measured amount daily. Intake can be restricted by moving the barrier slowly or increased by faster progression up the clamp.

Parlour concentrates - purchased concentrates are often fed in feeders in the parlour. Measured out according to yield, usually at 0.4 kgs of concentrate per kg of milk produced over that supplied by the basal ration.

OUTSIDER'S GUIDE

KEY NUTRITION FACTS

Concentrate use/cow/year	1.4 tonnes
use/litre of milk	0.25 kg.

Silage density in clamps:

dry matter 20%	725 kg fresh wt/m³
25%	660 kg
30%	617 kg

Estimation of **silage** dry matter: take some and squeeze in the hand, if:

juice readily expressed	< 20% dry matter
juice expressed with difficulty	20 to 25%
no juice expressed, but hands moist	> 25%

Big bales. Their weight depends on size and dry matter content. e.g. for 1.2m diameter bales:

dry matter 30%	500 - 550 kgs fresh weight.
20%	550 - 600 kgs

Typical Forage Crop Yields

Crop		Tonnes/ha	% D.M.
Turnips	tops	15 - 30	5.0 - 7.5
	roots	60 - 80	1.5-3.0
Kale	autumn	70	8
	winter	50	7
Fodder beet	tops	35	3 - 6
	roots	60 - 90	10 - 14
Rye	early grazing	750 - 2250 kg of D.M.	
	silage	16 - 40	22
Forage maize		30	35

NUTRITION

DRINKING WATER

KEY FACTS

- ☛ Cow needs 10 - 70 litres/day.

- ☛ Affected by herbage, dry matter and weather.

- ☛ Peak drinking period is early evening to sundown, up to 50 % in 3 hours!

- ☛ Drinking rate can be 15 - 20 litres/minute per cow.

- ☛ Troughs and water delivery are critical:

> **water shortage = thirsty cows = less milk**

GRAZING

Ideally grass should be maintained at a height of 8-10 cm, to prevent overgrazing and slow growth, or undergrazing and low nutritional value, both of which lead to decreased milk yields.

Paddock Grazing

4 0.95 ha paddocks to hold 100 cows/days	3	2	1 moveable water through
gangway for cows			
5	6	7	8

The field is divided into paddocks of the same size. Grass takes about 21 days to reach grazing stage. Allow 0.2 ha of grass per dairy cow from April to September.

When growth is slow bring a reserve area of grass into the system.

This system provides fresh grass when it is at the young leafy stage (highest D value); maintenance plus 18-23 litres of milk per day. The grass recovers quickly from being grazed and allows intensive stocking. However, long leys are needed, the cost of fencing can be high and fences that are not permanent can be broken by the cows, and labour requirement for repairs can be high.

NUTRITION

Strip Grazing

unrgazed area

forward electric fence

back fence

water

grazed area
(recovering)

The most efficient form of grazing for the smaller herd. The cows are given access to a limited area of fresh grass twice daily, or for longer periods by the forward movement of an electric fence.

A back fence is used to fence off the area that has been grazed. There must be room for all the stock at the feeding face and a 'run back' gives the stock room to exercise. Water must be available. A dense sward (20 cm high) should carry about 70 cows per 0.4ha per day.

Zero Grazing

The grass is cut and carted to the stock which is kept in yards. This gives flexibility to the type of forage to be fed e.g. maize, sugar beet tops.

There is no wastage due to dung, treading etc. and the stocking density can be increased. Distant fields and unfenced fields can be used to provide grass. However, the system is more expensive especially in machinery and labour and there may be a slurry problem.

Set Stocking

A fixed number of stock are grazed on the field all season (not necessarily in the same area), at a moderate stocking rate. A stocking rate of 5 cows/ha or 4 cows/ha in spring calving herds. However, this may vary if the cows are given access to alternative grazing when grass growth slows.

Extensive Grazing

A fixed head of cows is carried on a given area, regardless of the seasonal variation in grass output. The grass is overstocked in summer and understocked in spring and early autumn. The sward suffers and the stock do not obtain full benefit from grazing.

Buffered Grazing

When grass growth is restricted (by drought or cold) a 'buffer' is supplied to maintain cow dry matter intake and to prevent overgrazing. The buffer may be silage, grass, spring barley straw or ammonia treated wheat straw. The buffer is given after milking before the cows are turned out to graze, or at grass.

Buffered grazing allows tight early season stocking; increased conservation and less worry over summer droughts; better and more consistent yields and more efficient use of the forage area.

HEALTH

INTRODUCTION

Great pressures are put on modern dairy cows by the high level of productivity asked of them. Consequently, most diseases are caused by a combination of factors which include management, nutrition, stockmanship, environment and infection. Mastitis, lameness and poor fertility comprise 80% of all cattle diseases. Prevention and control are more important than treatment.

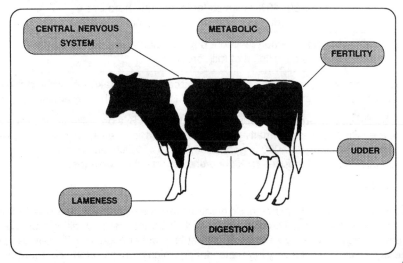

Vaccination

Calfhood vaccination is commonly done to avoid *E. coli*, Salmonella, viral scours and pneumonia. Adult vaccination continues with annual boosters for such diseases as *Leptospira hardjo*, one of the major causes of abortion in dairy cows.

Fertility

Factors that are all associated with prolonged calving intervals, anoestrus and foetal reabsorption include:

infectious diseases	Leptospirosis, Brucellosis
infection / hormonal / behavioural conditions	anoestrous, silent-heat, continuous heat (nymphomaniac cow)
metabolic imbalance	low blood sugar, poor dietary protein levels and mineral/vitamin imbalance. Over 1/3 of cows are culled as a result of poor fertility.

HEALTH

Mastitis   (udder infection)

20% of culled cows are due to this usually bacterial infection which damages milk-forming tissues, leading to a yield reduction in liquids, solids and results in the release of inflammatory ('somatic') cells.

Forms:	Effects & symptoms
Clinical	visible signs, swollen udder, hardness, changes in milk. 30 -40% cows suffer in average herd every lactation due to bacteria or milking machine defects
Subclinical	udder damage without physical signs. 10-20 million somatic cells/ml of milk produced

Treatment is by infusion of antibiotics, and great care must be taken to withhold milk from public supplies. Prevention and control involve all round quality herd management.

Somatic cell counts are carried out weekly by the M.M.B,'s on bulk milk to indicate infection levels. Premium and penalty payments system is used to encourage disease control. A count less than 200,000 is good, 200,000 to 400,000 leaves room for improvement and above 400,000 reduces milk price and represents a yield loss.

Ketosis (Acetonaemia)

Usually occuring in early lactation. So named due to the high levels of ketones (of which one is acetone) in the blood. The cow is dull, off its food and loses condition fast . Caused by extreme energy deficiency as the cow is unable to get enough from its diet, causing it to utilize its own body fat at a very high rate, during which process ketones are formed and if they occur at a very high level in the blood the cow becomes unwell.

Usually occuring in early lactation, prevention requires reassessment of the whole herd diet and management. A high intake of dietary energy can also lead to metabolic acidosis or ketosis when liver tissues cannot cope with the recycling of ketones into glucose and glycine.

Milk Fever (calcium deficiency nervous disorder)

Hypocalcaemia usually occurs within a day or two following calving with the cow being dull, uncoordinated and cold, before going down, and unless treated comatose and dead within hours.

Caused by the cow switching calcium to udder rather than uterus while failing to mobilize enough with sufficient speed from body reserves. Treated by farmers giving subcutaneous calcium borogluconate injection. Prevention by dietary management in the dry period to stimulate calcium mobilization mainly with high magnesium, low calcium diet.

HEALTH

Staggers (Grass Staggers)

Due to low blood magnesium (hypomagnesaemia) cow becomes nervous, twitchy, off food. If untreated goes down with convulsions and death in a few minutes. Cow may be mildly affected for days. Frequently occurs with high yielding milkers at spring grass who are unable to absorb dietary magnesium. Vet should always be called and prevention can be difficult.

Lameness

Again 20% of cows are culled due to this condition, and 20% are affected every year; causes loss of condition, milk yield and fertility. Many causes responsible including lack of comfortable lying time in cubicles, large single concentrate feeds especially those high in starch and poor feeding and housing during rearing of young stock. **Laminitis** is caused when swollen foot tissue is unable to expand due to horny outer layers.

OTHER DISEASES

B.V.D. (Bovine Viral Diarrhoea / Mucosal Disease)

A disease transmitted to calves during pregnancy. It affects the immune system. Calves which survive can pass it on to others when they join the milking herd. Such carriers can be undetected and the condition can build up to epidemic proportions with an abortion or scour 'storm'.

NOTIFIABLE DISEASES

Farmers must inform the Ministry of the following diseases:

Tuberculosis

Originally a severe problem in humans. T.B. has now virtually been eradicated from the British Isles. Infected cattle are slaughtered or disposed of. In addition, all herds are tested under the Attested Herd Scheme.

Cattle are now tested every three years and any reactors found are slaughtered, with compensation paid to the owners. Producer - Retailers are tested every twelve months.

HEALTH

Anthrax

A very rare disease. The main symptom being death. Any unexplained death must be tested.

Brucellosis

Milk and blood testing identifies reactor cows. All abortions must be checked. Positive confirmed reactors are slaughtered.

Foot and Mouth Disease

A virus disease causing blisters on the feet and tongue of cloven-footed animals. Frothing of the mouth and lameness are the classic symptoms. A viral infection which has been eradicated by slaughtering all infected animals since the early 1930's. Last major outbreak was in 1967-68 with minor occurrences on the Isle of Wight and in Dorset/ Hampshire in early 1970's.

Bovine Spongiform Encephalopathy (B.S.E.)

Appeared in dairy cows in the late 1980's. It is thought to have evolved from the Scrapie agent in sheep, taking several years to develop clinical symptoms which result from degeneration of the nervous system. The cow is unable to control muscles, becomes aggressive, and seems to go "mad". Hence the colloquial name 'Mad Cow Disease'.

Control is by slaughter with compensation (100% since February 1990) for clinically affected animals. No tests for sub-clinical stages are available.

Enzootic Bovine Leucosis

Enlargement of the lymph nodes with associated weight loss and poor production. Notifiable since 1977, affected animals eventually die. Cows are blood tested and a register of E.B.L. free herds kept. They must be E.B.L. free to be used in bull studs or for export of embryos or breeding stock.

LEGAL ASPECTS

Codes For The Use Of Medicines

i Source

Obtain products only from veterinary surgeons or registered agricultural merchants.

ii   Storage

Temperature and light can be critical. Some products must be kept under lock and key.

iii Records

Records must be kept of purchases and use (date, quantity, stock). In some cases empty bottles must be returned to the supplier.

iv Withdrawal times

Withdrawal periods are laid down for specific products relating to the time between the end of the treatment and the date of slaughter or sale of milk.

It is important to avoid certain residues in meat and milk for human consumption. This is especially so when intramammary antibiotics are used which can potentially contaminate the milk. The processors impose strong sanctions against contamination, the sensitivtiy of the current test for the presence of 'inhibitory substances' in milk corresponds to **0.006 ppm of penicillin.**

v   Mixing medicines in feed

If medicines are to be included in feed in mixes made **on the farm,** the farm must register with the Royal Pharmaceutical Society of Great Britain and purchase an annual licence from them to do so.

Cattle Identifications (1994)

All cows must carry two approved ear tags with the same identification number and the holding number. Animals must be tagged from 36 hours of age to 7 days. Detailed records must be kept on the farm and all animals need this document with movement records when going for sale. Records must be kept for 10 years.

HEALTH

INTRODUCTION

The dairy cow spends from 3 to 7 months in winter quarters and the rest of the year out grazing in fields. As well as winter quarters, a dairy unit will need a milking parlour and associated facilities, feed stores, calving and health care accommodation, holding yards, office and storage facilities. Storage and handling of slurry, especially for a large herd is a major consideration.

A Typical Dairy Unit

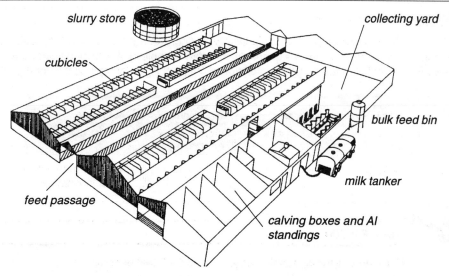

slurry store

collecting yard

cubicles

bulk feed bin

milk tanker

feed passage

calving boxes and AI standings

TYPES OF ACCOMMODATION

Cubicles

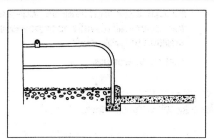

Metal divisions under an umbrella roof giving cows individual living areas. Cubicle dimensions and flooring are variable being related to cow size and farmers' pockets!

Kennels

These are on the same principle as cubicles i.e. each cow has her own lying area but costs are considerably less overall. The cubicle is set in concrete under an umbrella roof, the kennel forms part of the building structure.

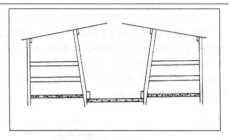

Siting And Layout Of Cubicles

This includes easy cow access to silage or to feeding areas and as close to fodder stores as conditions permit. Cubicles are generally arranged in single or double parallel rows, and head to head or tail to tail all within an enclosed building. Approximate dimensions (m):

Length	Width	Size of stall divisions	
	between divisions	height above heelstone	length
2.05 -2.15	1.05 - 1.175	1.0 - 1.15	to within 150mm of fall of heelstone

KEY FACTS

Floor area including feeding area	6.5 - 7.5m² per cow
Width of passage between rows	2.4m
Cross passages every	20 cubicles
Sawdust, wood chippings or chopped straw **bedding**	3 - 7 kg per cow per week
Ventilation is natural	through a continuous open ridge and the upper half of walls open boarded in addition to gable ends
Lighting is	natural or artificial

Loose Yard Layout

In part-covered yards, open area should face South or South-east.

HOUSING

Space requirements include:

Age of animal	Lying or bedding area (m²)	Loafing or feeding area (m²)	Manger length per beast (mm)
6 months	1.8 - 2.8	-	300 - 450
1 year	2.8 - 3.7	-	450 - 550
Adult cows	3.7 - 4.7	1.8 - 2.3	600 - 700

MILKING PARLOURS

Main types include :

cowshed
abreast
herringbone
rotary :   **abreast**
                 herringbone

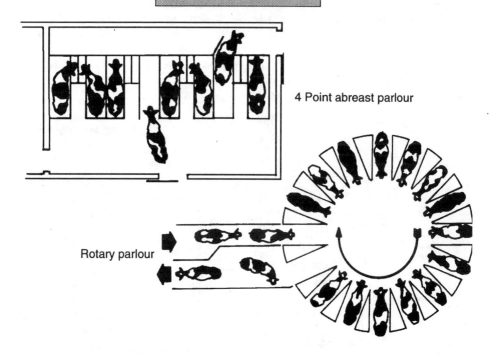

4 Point abreast parlour

Rotary parlour

HOUSING

The Herringbone

Cows stand with their head at the outside wall, usually with a feed trough for concentrate feeding. The milker stands in a central pit 1.1 to 1.3 metres wide and 0.6m below cow floor level.

A one-man parlour may be an automated 8 x 4 or 10 x 5 (ten cows sharing five milking units). With automatic cluster removal a single man can manage up to a 14 x 14 layout. The herringbone has the advantage of a fast throughput - average 1 to 1.5 minutes per cow over the whole milking time. This means that for an 8 x 8 parlour, each batch of cows is in the parlour for 8 to 12 minutes.

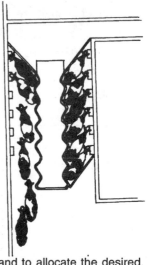

Parlour Automation

Cows may be given **transponder** collars to wear. These have the cow's identity coded into a radio receiver - transmitter. As she puts her head into the feed trough, a signal is received which allows parlour computer systems to identify the cow and to allocate the desired amount of feed in relation to the milk yield. This system allows the milk yield to be monitored at every milking.

Automatic cluster removers (A.C.R.) take off clusters once a cow has finished milking. Teat sprays (against mastitis infection) can be set up in an exit race and even a weigh pad can be inserted so that cows are weighed individually.

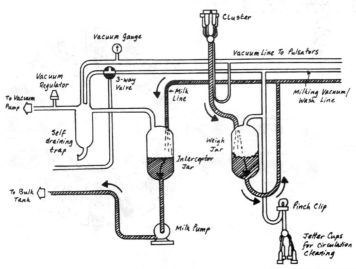

Servicing Of Milking Equipment

It is essential that all equipment is regularly serviced to ensure accurate vacuum pressure for milking. Too great a pressure causes damage to the cows teats.

Some systems use wide bore milk liner with no weigh jar, especially in fully automated systems.

HOUSING

Typical Milking Routine For An Automated Herringbone Parlour

Action	Time per cow (mins)
Let cows in	0.10
Identify and feed concentrates	0.05
Dry wipe teats with soft paper towel	0.15
Put clusters on	0.20
Automatic cluster removal	
Teat dip with iodophor/emollient disinfectant	0.10
Let cows out and transfer milk to bulk vat in dairy	0.10
Miscellaneous	0.05
Total	**0.75 minutes / cow**

Total Throughput 10 x 10 parlour

10 cows x 0.75 minutes / cow

= 7.5 minutes per batch

= 8 batches per hour

= 80 cows per hour

CALVING ACCOMMODATION

In the ideal unit cows will calve in individual loose boxes. For 100 cows calving over two months, this means 5 - 8 boxes allowing for some cows to stay on using them as sick pens. A typical calving box would be 20 - 25 m² floor area, accessible by tractor loader, well strawed with good ventilation, and drinking water supply.

GENERAL DESIGN PRINCIPLES

Any dairy unit should take note of the five flows of dairying:

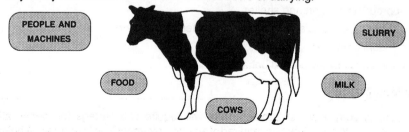

PEOPLE AND MACHINES

SLURRY

FOOD

MILK

COWS

Movement is from or to the cows. Each flow should avoid crossing over or mixing with the others.

HOUSING

GUIDE TO HOUSING COSTS

Kennels	£280 / cow place
Cubicles	£490 / cow place
Open loose yard building	£110 / m² floor area
Milking parlour	10 x 10 £60K - £100, 000

LEGAL REQUIREMENTS

The Water Act 1989

The Water Act 1989 tries to prevent water pollution happening and allows people to be prosecuted if they cause pollution. Under Section 107 of the Water Act 1989 it is an offence to cause or knowingly permit a discharge of poisonous, noxious or polluting matter into any "controlled waters" without proper authority.

There are many husbandry considerations with regard to the application of slurry; the above merely cover the more important legal aspects.

Other Acts Relating To Pollution

Collection and Disposal of Water Regulations 1988.

Control of Pollution (Silage, Slurry and Agricultural Fuel Oil) Regulations 1991.

The Cow Welfare Code

While this is only a code of practice it has the approval of Parliament. Anyone found breaking the code and causing distress to cows, may be prosecuted. The code takes account of the basic needs of cows viz:

☞ freedom from thirst, hunger and malnutrition

☞ appropriate comfort and shelter

☞ prevention/diagnosis and treatment of disease and injury

☞ freedom from fear

☞ freedom to display normal behaviour

Animal Identification

All animals born after 1st January 1994 will require two eartags for identification purposes. Adequate records will be required of animal movement, death and sale. A holding number will be allocated.

REPRODUCTION

INTRODUCTION

The **profitability** of a herd relies on **reproductive efficiency**. This requires the accurate observation of heat periods ensuring that the target calving period of 365 days is achieved, thus maximising milk production. Failure to detect heat periods results in an overall reduction in milk yield.

To give maximum lifetime yield one calving per year is required over the productive cow's life of 4 to 8 years. Fertility and lactation has a major influence on profitability.

KEY ASSESSMENT QUESTIONS

Average herd targets	
Calving to calving interval	365 days
Calving to conception interval	85 days
Gestation period	280 - 288 days
Average serves per conception	1.6
Average conception rate to 1st service	60 - 68%
Days from calving to first service	42 days
*Condition score at calving	3 to 3.5
Condition score at service	2.75 to 3.0

*Depends on calving season and pattern required.

KEY FACTS

Dairy Cow Heat Periods And Service

☛ Heat cycles start approximately 21 days after calving and repeat every 18 to 24 days until the cow conceives.

☛ Heat lasts 6 to 36 hrs, with an average of 24 hrs, depending on time of year, cow age and body condition. For best conception rates using A.I., service should be in the last third of the heat period.

☛ Heat is seen as a change in cow behaviour.

REPRODUCTION

Heat Cycle

During **pre-oestrus** the progesterone level is down and the oestrogen level is rising. The cow's behaviour is as follows:

i   cow licking and sniffing others

ii   cow's chin resting on others' backs or shoulders

ii   cow uneasy and restless

iv   cow off her food and standing with others on heat in a small group away from the herd

Standing cow is on heat

Once **oestrus** is established and the oestrogen level is at a maximum:

i   cow mounts another from behind, cow underneath stands still if on "active heat"; if cow underneath is not on heat it rejects mounting

ii   cow mounts another from the front, cow on top is on heat

iii "mooing continuously" as if calling for a bull

iv   may be a clear mucus discharge hanging from the vulva (the "bulling string")

Cow rejects mounting and is not on heat

One of these cows may be on heat

Post-oestrus. The oestrogen level falls and progesterone level rises. If insemination has been unsuccessful the cow returns to anoestrus.

REPRODUCTION

KEY POINTS

☞ Heat periods must be recorded.

☞ The cows must be easily identified.

☞ Routine observations must be made.

Farmers Routine For On-heat cows

Genus runs a National A.I. service in liaison with private breeders and a number of other commercial A.I. Centres.

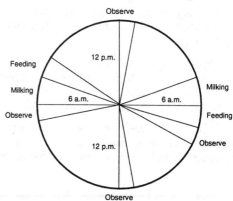

i   The cow is seen to be on heat.

ii The herdsman using A.I. will call for the inseminator.

The herdsman will indicate the bull required or a "bull of the day" may be used. The desired bull breed and name has been chosen originally from an A.I. catalogue in order to maintain or to improve the quality of the herd in some desired characteristics.

iii Once inseminated, an A.I. Certificate is left by the Inseminator confirming the identity of the cow and of the bull from which the semen had been collected.

Semen can also be ordered by the farm in advance of the breeding season and stored ready for use at the depot, or on the farm. On some farms "Do it Yourself A.I." is carried out by a trained member of the farm staff.

Number Of Inseminations By Country And Breed ('000's)

	England & Wales	Scotland	N. Ireland
Ayrshire	13	7	0.8
All dairy	1181	93	68
Beef breeds	643	64	117

Source: Dairy Facts & Figures, 1993.

Reproductive Efficiency

A cow should produce a calf annually at a time dictated by the farmer. In practice only 85% of cows calve annually. This is due to a failure to breed as well as poor heat detection and conception rates.

REPRODUCTION

PREGNANCY DIAGNOSIS

Ensuring cows are in calf through diagnosis, enables problem animals to be detected early. **Infertility costs money - £3.00 to £5.00 for each day** added to calving interval over the 365 day target.

After 24 days a milk progesterone test is carried out on the farm using kits, or is performed by the M.M.B. and other laboratories. High progesterone levels mean the cow is in calf at that stage. Later reabsorption is possible, so the pregnancy needs to be confirmed by rectal palpation carried out by a veterinary surgeon.

Several other pregnancy diagnosis tests are available, based on the use of **Ultra Sound**. A probe is inserted in the rectum and ultrasound is bounced back from the increased blood flowing through the uterine arteries.

CALVING

Target: easy calving, lively calf, 30 - 45 kg liveweight, fast recovery for the cow so that a maximum milk yield is given.

Because calving performance can affect the health of the cow for several weeks afterwards, breeding organisations publish calving performance details for bulls tested.

Points To Consider

- ☛ Select an easy calving sire
- ☛ Record service date accurately
- ☛ Feed pregnant cows correctly

Gestation Periods For Various Breeds

Breed	Gestation length (days)
Fresian	280
Limousin	288
Blonde'	286
Charolais	285
Simmental	287
Hereford	283
Belgian Blue	284

REPRODUCTION

LACTATION

Key Facts

Type of system: cows calving between October and January have lactation yields up to 600kg higher than cows calving at other times (due to the length of lactation and the spring rise in production when the cows are turned out to grass).

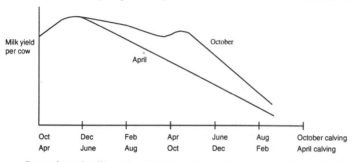

Lactation peak: the higher the peak of lactation the faster the rate of decline, however, usually the higher the peak the higher the total yield. The peak is usually determined by nutritional restraints.

Quantity of milk : this depends on the supply of nutrients from the diet, the supply of nutrients from the body reserve and the hormonal control of partitioning the dietary nutrients between the mammary gland and other body tissue.

Feeding: feeding a fixed rate of concentrates throughout a herd's lactation period (flat rate feeding) results in a lower yield peak but lactation lasts longer. Total yield is not affected.

Pregnancy: if a cow is in calf about 85 days post calving, the milk production decline accelerates to give a total lactation length of 305 days, allowing 60 day dry period.

Dry period: this allows a cow to replace body nutrients, restore the secretory tissue of the udder, build-up the body reserves and allows the unborn calf to develop.

"Milking off her back" occurs when the high yielding cow mobilises body reserves to produce high quantities of milk early in lactation.

HEALTHY HEIFER REARING

Minimise the incidence of disease infection, especially pneumonia, during the first winter. During the second winter, house in groups well matched in size, in accomodation similar to that which they will live in as adult cows .

To minimise stress before heifers enter the herd 'formally', get them familiar with the cubicles and the milking parlour well before they calve.

REPRODUCTION

KEY ASSESSMENT QUESTIONS

The figures below are **not** national averages, but those taken from A.B.C., 1994.

Physical details	Targets	
Milk yield (litres/cow/year)	5550	
Concentrate use (kg/cow)	1499	
Concentrate use (kg/litre)	0.27	
Margin over concentrates(£)	937	
Stocking rate (L.S.U./ha)	2.1	
Nitrogen use (kg/ha)	220	
Replacement rate (%)	22.5	
Milk price (pence/litre)	23	
Concentrate (£/tonne)	142	(average of purchased concentrates and straights)
Cull cow value (£)	525	

GROSS MARGIN BUDGET/COW

	£
Annual milk sales	1277
Calf sales/value (mortality etc. allowed for)	120
Herd depreciation	122
Output (£/cow)	**1275**
Variable costs:	
concentrates	213
purchased bulk feeds	20
forage cost/cow	81
sundries; vet & med, quota	105
Total variable costs (£/cow)	**419**
Gross margin/cow(£)	856
Gross margin/ha (£)	1797

PERFORMANCE

FIXED COSTS

Profitable farms manage to minimise fixed costs, and to maximise output from their type of farming system so that fixed costs per unit output are as low as possible.

The figures below are typical levels of fixed costs for specialist dairy farms. These are shown for farms of different sizes. Individual farms will vary in their levels of fixed costs for specific reasons - e.g. new farms will have high **rental charges of 40% to 70%** higher than those quoted. **Larger farms** will tend to have lower costs/hectare.

Farm Type	TOTAL FIXED COSTS (£/ha)		
	<50 ha	50 - 100 ha	>100 ha
Specialist Dairy more than 75% gross output from dairying	1260	1050*	875

Source: A.B.C.

Fixed cost elements

*The table below shows the components of these fixed costs:

Item - Specialist Dairy	£/ha
Regular labour	435
Depreciation	145
Repairs, tax and insurance - equipment	90
Fuel and electricity	65
Contract charges - hedging/ditching	25
Land maintenance	40
Rent & rates	160
Fixed costs sundries	90
TOTAL	**1050**

For further details of prices under the quota system, see Support ( ).

OUTSIDER'S GUIDE

QUOTAS

The price of milk is supported through a national and EU quota scheme. The quota system (started in 1984) controlled the total supply of milk by the imposition of a production quota on each farm. The individual farm quota was the farm's 1983 production less 9%. Since then further reductions have been made. The effect of this constraint is to maintain prices received by those still in production. A cut of 1% in quota was made for 1992/93. A further cut of 1% applies to the 1993/94 production year.

The basic Milk Target Price for the 1994-95 milk year is 21.6p/litre. The Intervention Price for butter is £2323.58 per tonne, and for skimmed milk powder it is £1567.49 per tonne.

LEVIES

Co-responsibility Levy

The milk target price is 21.96 p/litre, however there is a co-responsibility levy on milk sold to the M.M.B'.s which is charged to the wholesale producers. This levy was abolished on 1st April 1993.

The Super Levy

The super levy that is payable on milk produced over quota is 28.97 p/litre.

Other Payments

i   Hygiene bands (quality payment scheme on total bacteria count (T.B.C.) (see 🏷️).

ii   Bulk milk cell count (quality scheme on herd mastitis levels).

iii Seasonality payment for July to October, paid in December.

iv   Rolling fund payment (return of co-operative profits to farmers) paid in March.

PERFORMANCE

THE
OUTSIDER'S GUIDE
to
EGGS

1995 Edition

PRODUCTION

PRODUCTION IN THE EU

Two years of expansion within the Egg sector of the EU Poultry Industry have led to over production and the problems associated with it during 1992. Production has been cut back and this will last into 1994. The production of 1993 was 2251 million eggs less than its peak in 1991. The EU.egg output has back by 2.7% since 1991. Consumption is also down but expots of eggs to non EU countries was up by 29% in 1993.

Over the last 10 years per capita consumption has fallen by 25 eggs. Net exports fell by 10% in 1992. Chick placings in the EU for 1992 were down 8.6 million to 249.1 million a reduction of 3.3%. While for the U.K. alone this dropped 0.9 million to 31.8 million or 2.75%

Across the EU the returns for eggs have in general been better during 1993. In the UK. they remained firm during the Spring 0f 1994 falling into the red again during the Summer. It bottomed out and started to climb again and with the better feed prices of Autumn the prospects are better.

EU Egg Production (millions)

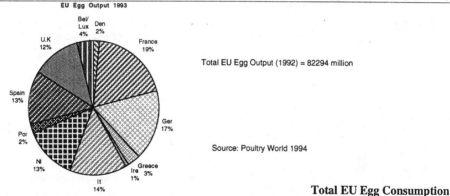

Total EU Egg Output (1992) = 82294 million

Source: Poultry World 1994

Total EU Egg Consumption

Egg production in Europe has decreased overall from 1981-1991 by 1.2%.

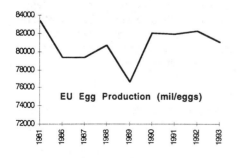

Average egg **consumption** is down by 3 eggs/capita in the EU from 1992 and net E.U. egg exports to non EU countries was down by 10% on 90-91. Average 1993 egg consumption is down 3 eggs/capita in the UK to 172. Whilst the general trend is downwards, per capita consumption was up in some countries especially in Denmark where consumption has increased from 229 to 253 eggs/capita over the last 10yrs.

PRODUCTION

UNITED KINGDOM PRODUCTION

Egg production output in 1992 was valued at about £405 million in contrast to broiler production at about £1047m.

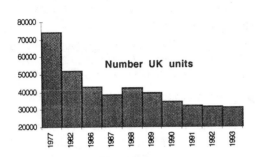

Number Of Laying Flocks In The UK

In the 10 years up to 1992, the national flock size had decreased as had the number of flocks. However, as with other enterprises, the proportion of larger flocks in the national flock increased steadily .

Flock Size (% Of Total Flock)

The Salmonella scare of 1989 and the conditions placed upon the UK laying flock will do nothing to change the situation. The flock will be in the hands of even fewer producers. At present only the UK flock is under stringent health regulations but in a short time the rest of Europe should fall in line.

Production

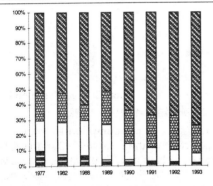

The national flock is generally of birds housed intensively, about 85% being in cages, the remaining 15% on deep litter and free range.

Growing pressure from the welfare lobby could well cause cages to be banned as has happened already in some EU countries and a return to the less intensive methods. At present the market is stronger for eggs produced in these systems, but it should be remembered that the production costs are higher and as more are produced the premiums will diminish.

Market

The market in the UK is nearly 100% brown eggs. However, there is a small demand for white eggs from certain ethnic groups and from some caterers (who claim white eggs shell better).

OUTSIDER'S GUIDE

Consumption

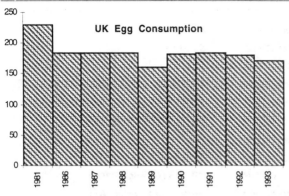

Egg consumption in the UK fell over the last 10 years from 216 - 172 per person/yr. The low figure for 1989 was due to the salmonella scare which caused egg consumption to fall by approximately 12%.

Approximately 3.30 eggs are consumed (person/wk) with nearly 2 are eaten as egg.

Cost Of Egg Production (p/dozen)

The declining trend over the last 10 years 1978-1991 has been caused by poor returns and high costs. Production has always been cyclic and although in 1990 prices were good the risks are high. As always, high prices will once again attract increased UK output and imports and force prices down.

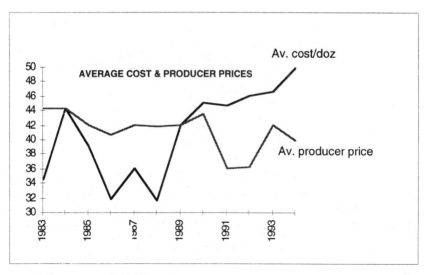

Source: Poultry World September 1994

PRODUCTION

KEY ASSESSMENT QUESTIONS

Average Nº eggs produced/hen	290 (24.16 dozen)
Typical weeks of laying	52 to 56
Peak production	95%
Food consumption/hen for the laying period	41.975 kg (i.e. 115g/hen/day X 365)
Food consumed/dozen eggs	1.74kg (i.e. food conversion ratio)
Food cost/hen	£6.50 (£155 per tonne)
Bird depreciation	£2.10
Gross margin/hen	£2.99 (@ 48p/dozen)
Gross margin/dozen eggs	£0.123 (@ 48p/dozen)
Average % production	80% (see page 147)

Eggs must be graded before sale, unless sold directly to consumer at farm gate.

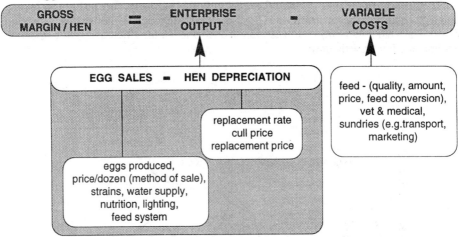

GROSS MARGIN / HEN = ENTERPRISE OUTPUT - VARIABLE COSTS

EGG SALES - HEN DEPRECIATION

replacement rate
cull price
replacement price

eggs produced,
price/dozen (method of sale),
strains, water supply,
nutrition, lighting,
feed system

feed - (quality, amount,
price, feed conversion),
vet & medical,
sundries (e.g.transport,
marketing)

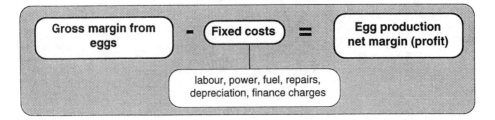

Gross margin from eggs - Fixed costs = Egg production net margin (profit)

labour, power, fuel, repairs,
depreciation, finance charges

PRODUCTION

PRODUCTION CYCLE

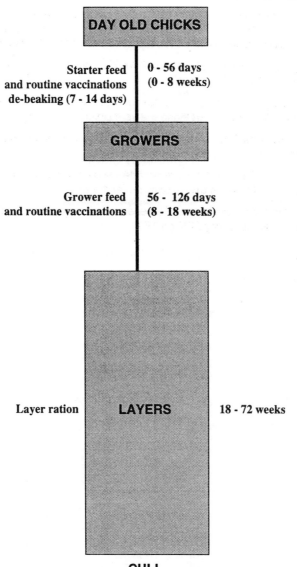

DAY OLD CHICKS

Starter feed
and routine vaccinations
de-beaking (7 - 14 days)

0 - 56 days
(0 - 8 weeks)

GROWERS

Grower feed
and routine vaccinations

56 - 126 days
(8 - 18 weeks)

Layer ration   **LAYERS**   **18 - 72 weeks**

CULL

MARKETING

INDUSTRY COMMENTARY 1994

After hitting a low of 26p/dozen in July 1992 the egg market recovered in the second half of the year, peaking at 44p/dozen in December 1992. The price fell again in the spring of 1993 but recovered and stabilised at about 42p/dozen during the Summer.

Chick placings in the UK for 1993 were up 0.4 million or 1.25%. Placings for the EU 12 were also up by 8.4 million to 257.1 million.

The average Packer to Producer Price during 1993 was some 22% better than 1992. The last 3 quarters being better than those the year before.

The Packer to Producer Price for the 1st six moths was 10% up on on the same period of 1993. Feed prices from the Spring of 1994 have eased.

Egg prices slipped in May 1994 but have made a recovery during the autumn and feed prices have again eased down to give slightly better margin.

This could lead to over production and a general decrease in prices, although exports to Non EU countries are up nearly 30% on 1992.

MARKETING

MAIN PRODUCTS

There is only one product involved, that is the egg, which is extremely versatile. End of lay (E.O.L.) birds are sold for processing into soup, pie meat, etc.

MARKET OUTLETS

Although there is only one main product, there are a number of outlets through which it can be distributed.

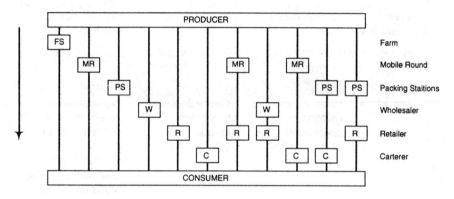

The farm shop and the mobile round are operations carried out direct from the farm and are now becoming increasingly popular forms of outlet.

UK International Trade ('000 Cases)

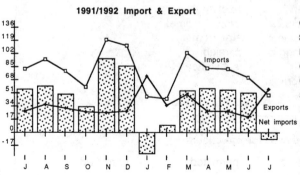

1991/1992 Import & Export

Eggs can be exported to other countries, but there are strict rules with which the farmer must comply if he wishes to export. The UK was a net exporter of some 240 million shell eggs in 1992. The EU was a net exporter of 1350 million shell eggs in 1993.

Eggs must be graded before sale, unless sold directly to consumer at farm gate. They are graded for quality and size.

MARKETING

Varieties And Markets

Brown eggs are the main product, making up more than 95% of the market. White eggs, imports, reject eggs and other unsaleable eggs make up the rest.

Quality And Standard

The quality of the egg is important if it is to be marketable. EU marketing standards for eggs are as follows:

	Class A	Class B	Class C
Shell & membrane	normal, clean, intact	normal, intact	may be visibly cracked
Air cell	not exceeding 6mm in depth, stationary	not exceeding 9mm in depth	may be 9mm
Egg white	clear, translucent gelatinous consistency, free of any foreign substances	clear translucent, free of any foreign substance	includes all eggs which do not satisfy the requirements of Classes A and B, but are suitable for manufacturing food-stuffs for human consumption
Yolk	visible under candling as a shadow only, without apparent contour, not moving from its central position when the egg is rotated, free from any foreign substances	visible under candling as a shadow only (not required with eggs stored in lime) free from any foreign substances	
Embryo	no perceptible development		
Smell	free of all foreign odours		
Wet or Dry-cleaning	not permitted	permitted	permitted

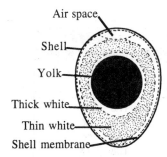

Air space

Shell

Yolk

Thick white

Thin white

Shell membrane

All eggs which do not fall into Classes A, B or C are classed as "Industrial Eggs" and may not be used for human consumption, either in the manufacture of foodstuffs of otherwise.

Extra Quality

These are eggs which are very fresh and under one week old when sold.

Egg Characteristics

Shell colour varies from white to deep brown with an occasional 'speckled' shell, depending on the breed of bird. Colour can influence consumer choice.

Yolk colour can also influence consumer choice. Yolk colour is measured using a standard colour sequence on what is known as the Roche Scale, which ranges from a pale lemon colour to a deep orange. Most consumers prefer an in-between colour of dark orange, number 10-12 on Roche Scale. The producer can influence yolk colour by including feedstuffs like grass meal, lucerne, maize and/or artificial pigment.

Egg Sizes

Eggs must be graded before sale, unless sold directly to consumer at farm gate. They are graded for quality and size.

Size 0	75g+
1	70-75g
2	65-70g
3	60-65g
4	55-60g
5	50-55g
6	45-50g
7	<40g

MARKETING

Egg Grades, Sizes And Prices

Egg Price Indicators For week ending 28 August 1994, showing change on month					
p/doz	packer to producer		retailers buying price		high street shop price
Size 0	52.1	+3.9	103	nc	178	nc
Size 1	46.9	+2.2	101	nc	164	nc
Size 2	43.7	+1.3	93	nc	156	nc
Size 3	41.4	+0.7	88	nc	138	+4
Size 4	39.9	+0.1	83	nc	129	nc
Size 5	32.9	-0.3	71	NC	--	--
Free Range: Add premium of +35p (size 1-3)					

(Source: Poultry World)

Marketing Costs

Marketing costs include items such as egg boxes and package boxes. These are designed for protection, attractiveness and as a source of information for the customer. The boxes must state the egg size, packing date, name and address of packer, packing station number, number of eggs, class and the box must be effectively sealed. Free range eggs when sold other than to the packing station must be sold in prepacks with the packing date and marked 'Free Range'.

Egg Selling Features (Survey)

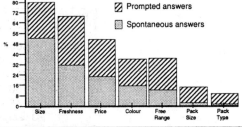

 LEGAL ASPECTS

In order to sell eggs as Class A, Size 1,2,3,4,5,6,7 the packer must be registered with M.A.F.F. eggs inspectorate. The packing station number is on all boxes. All UK packing stations have a number commencing 9.

Imported eggs can be repacked in the UK, they then carry the UK packing station number on the box making it impossible to distinguish foreign eggs.

BREEDS & SYSTEMS

INTRODUCTION

It is commonly believed that all breeds originated from the Red Jungle Fowl *GALLUS GALLUS*, but at least 3 other sub-species of wild fowl, all originating in the eastern tropics, may have been involved.

Today's commercial layers are said to originate from:

> White Leghorn
> Rhode Island Red
> New Hampshire Red
> Plymouth Rock

Considerable improvements in productive performance have been made in recent years. The commercial layer should be able to lay large numbers of eggs of a good quality and size, even colour (usually brown) on as little feed as possible.

BREEDING IMPROVEMENTS

The average annual egg production per adult bird has increased from 123 eggs in 1945-6, to 285+ eggs in 1992, a direct result of improved selective breeding methods and advances in our knowledge of nutrition.

The hybrid layer, which has been responsible for a great part in this increase, is produced by the mating together of two in-bred strains, giving hybrid vigour (heterosis) and a greater performance potential. The hybrid marketed is only one of many produced, the rest being of lesser value and discarded.

The Breeds

The main commercial breeds in the UK are all hybrid strains and usually take their name from the company which produced them: **Hisex Brown, ISA Brown, Hy-Line Brown, Shaver Brown.**

Systems Of Breeding

Inbreeding	mating together of closely related stock
Outbreeding	mating together of unrelated stock
Closed flock	breed within one flock and bring no new stock into the flock
Line breeding	one strain is used more than once during breeding

BREEDS & SYSTEMS

A
B } C
A } D
E
A } F } G = (offspring)
Commercial layer

> **Line breeding**: one strain is used more than once during breeding

> **Reciprocal recurrent selection breeding**
>
> is the selection of the best birds from a flock, and the breeding of these birds and then the breeding of the best offspring from these birds.

Selecting Laying And Breeding Birds

By using **sex linkage** the sex of the day old chick can be determined visually. With commercial pullets this is done by colour, the female birds being brown (gold) and the male birds being white (silver). To obtain sex linkage the female parent must have the dominant gene. A similar technique is used in broiler production using fast feathering (female) and slow feathering (male) genes.

Laying Flock

Because the stock that is used for egg production is made up of hybrids, there is no point in breeding from them. Production of commercial stock is left to the breeding companies who own the breeding stock.

OUTSIDER'S GUIDE

LAYING SYSTEMS

The EU marketing standards lay down production systems as follows:

Free range	Birds must have continuous daytime access to open-air runs which are mainly covered with vegetation and with a maximum stocking density of 1000 hens per hectare. Hen house conditions must comply with those of deep litter systems. Perches must be provided at a rate of 15cm/bird.
Semi-intensive	As for free range defined above.
Deep litter	Birds are kept in hen houses with a maximum stocking density of 17.1 kg/m² or 8 birds/m² of floor space. At least one third of the floor should be solid with a litter covering material such as straw, wood shavings, sand or turf. At least one quarter of the floor area should be used for collection of droppings. Where a roosting area is provided at the rate of 1m² /25 birds or 15 cm of perch space is provided; the stocking density can be increased to 11.7 birds/m² . All barn systems should have a scratching area.
Perchery (barn)	Eggs produced under the perchery system are called barn eggs. This is a variation of the deep litter system. It incorporates a series of perches and feeders at different levels and enables a higher stocking density of 25 birds/m² to be obtained. Perches must allow 15cms of perch per hen.

Additional details, plus specific information on intensive battery (cage) systems see

Alternative Production System

Normal production is 52 weeks in lay, however if this is extended more eggs will result and the eggs will also be larger. The extra costs will only be food, labour, etc. because the bird will not lose any more value and it becomes attractive to consider for these reasons. However consideration must be given to shell quality as this will deteriorate as time goes on and extending the production cycle must be planned in advance to take into account any replacements that may be on their way.

Another alternative is to induce moult. This is where production is halted early at about 60 weeks of age and the birds are then moulted using the house environment and feed changes, and brought in for a second period of production usually lasting about 35 weeks.

The advantages are as follows:

    i. it is cheaper to moult than buy P.O.L. replacement pullets

    ii. eases cash flow

    iii. larger eggs produced

    iv. has other advantages when pullets are in short supply.

The disadvantages are as follows:

    i. less eggs laid and house may not be fully used due to first year mortality

    ii. egg quality is poorer

    iii. not always successful.

NUTRITION

WATER

A proper water supply for layers is vital, for without a supply, one cannot expect to get the best from a laying flock. Eggs contain 66% water showing how important it is for laying birds. A shortage of water will be reflected by a reduction in egg size. If the shortage continues egg production will fall as well.

Water Requirements

Water is essential not just because it forms the greatest part of the egg, but also to help the birds eat their dry food, as an aid to digestion. In addition, water is vital for the normal metabolism of the bird enabling it to grow and live.

Water should be given **ad lib**, it should be clean and easily accessible. The drinkers should be level with the birds back to avoid spillage and to avoid contamination with shavings and droppings. As a rule of thumb, laying birds drink twice as much water in weight as food eaten.

e.g. Supplying 130g of food/day/bird requires also 260g (260ml) of water/bird.

Methods Of Providing Water

Water can be provided in many different ways. The methods differ according to the system in which the flock is kept:

Deep litter	Rainbow Cavelier
	Plasson
	14 inch diameter "bell" drinker
Battery cage system	Nipple Drinker
Free range	Trough Drinkers

Requirements of drinker space according to breeder company:

ISA Brown	10 large circular drinkers/1000 birds
Hy-Line Brown	2cm drinking trough length/pullet
Shaver Brown	5cm drinking trough length/pullet

NUTRITION

FEEDING

Day Old To Point Of Lay (0 to 8 weeks):

During the first period 0 - 7 or 8 weeks the chicks are fed on Chick Mash or Chick **Starter** Crumbs. Both are complete diets and have a nutritional breakdown as follows:

Crude protein	%	18.00
ME	MJ/kg	11.70
Lysine	%	0.90
Methionine	%	0.38
Calcium	%	0.90
Phosphorus	%	0.45
Sodium	%	0.15
Salt	%	0.37
Linoleic acid	%	1.00

Consumption over this period: **1.5 to 2.0 kg/bird.** Optimum house temperature 21°C plus 1.5% consumption for each 1°C below 21°C.

Source: Poultry World Dec. 1989

During the 7-8 week period consumption would be about 1.5-2.0 kgs/bird and the food should be given ad lib. In the initial stage, food should be provided in feeders on cardboard, and supplementary feeders provided to enable easy access to food.

Feeding From 8 to 18 Weeks:

The ration is now a **growers** ration and it has a lower nutritional value, providing enough energy for the birds needs i.e. maintenance. Food is given ad lib or it may be restricted. It has the following specification:

Crude protein	%	15.5
ME	MJ/kg	11.30
Lysine	%	0.65
Methionine	%	0.28
Calcium	%	0.80
Phosphorus	%	0.35
Sodium	%	0.14
Salt	%	0.37
Linoleic acid	%	0.85

Consumption over this period 4.0 to 5.0 kg/bird

Total for rearing is 6.0 to 7.0 kg/bird

NUTRITION

Feeding From 18 Weeks Until The End Of Lay:

During this period, **layers** mash is fed. Commencing 2 weeks before the first egg. This is done in order to get the birds used to the new ration before they lay. This ration has a higher level of protein and calcium than the growers diet. There are also slight differences in other nutrient levels.

Higher protein levels are required for egg production. Higher calcium levels enable the birds to produce strong shelled eggs without going off their legs. There is an additional pigment used to give dark yolk colour which at present is Apocarotenoic Ester and Canthaxanthin. This ration is fed **ad lib**.

Different layers rations are available:

	Ration type				
	Layer 18	**Layer 17**	**Layer 16**	**Free Range Summer**	**Winter**
Crude protein %	18.00	17.00	16.00	17.50	15.50
ME MJ/kg	11.50	11.40	11.30	11.30	12.00
Lysine %	0.85	0.78	0.72	0.77	0.64
Methionine %	0.42	0.38	0.35	0.37	0.30
Calcium %	4.20	4.00	4.20	4.00	4.20
Phosphorus %	0.35	0.32	0.30	0.32	0.25
Sodium %	0.15	0.15	0.15	0.15	0.15
Salt %	0.37	0.37	0.37	0.37	0.37
Linoleic acid %	1.40	1.25	1.25	1.25	1.00

The feed used will depend on conditions in the flock. Small birds, birds producing large numbers of eggs or birds under great stocking density all require higher protein % diets such as layer 18.

STORAGE OF RATIONS

Bagged food costs approximately £15/tonne more than bulk and incurs a labour cost in handling (possibly twice). It is also easily contaminated by rats and mice. The savings made by using bulk feed can pay for a storage bin in a very short time.

All food stuffs must be stored properly to avoid deterioration which would render it unsuitable for feeding to livestock.

Storage should:

i   be on wooden pallets, not directly on the cement floor
ii   in cool and dry places
iii not be under direct heat
iv   avoid direct sunlight and exposure to air or oxygen

NUTRITION

For Bulk Food

Inside the bulk food bin excessive heat could build up during hot summers. Therefore, the bulk food ordering should be done in small quantities to avoid long term storage within the bulk bin. Aim to order once per week and empty the system occasionally. Improper storage could cause the food to go rancid i.e. the oil or fat in the ration has oxidized. This will result in unwanted complications in the stock.

KEY FACTS

Average food consumption/day	115g (110g to 130g)
Food consumption for the laying period	115g x 365 41975g (41.975 kg)
No. eggs produced	270 (24.16 dozen)
Food consumed to produce 1 dozen eggs	1.73kg
Food conversion ratio	1.73kg:1 dozen eggs

STOCKING RATES

No matter which system is used for egg production, there are welfare aspects to be considered. Stocking rates ensure adequate space for all types of stock breeds and strains. Breeding companies provide their customers with guide lines for the feeding space that their birds require:

Breed	Feed space
ISA Brown	50m chain/1000 pullets
Shaver Brown	7.5cm/pullet

LEGAL ASPECTS

The Codes of Recommendation for Welfare of Livestock (Domestic Fowl) (M.A.F.F.) are only codes of practice, produced with the approval of Parliament. However, anyone found causing suffering or distress to poultry may be prosecuted. Stocking densities should not be exceeded. (See 🖐.)

PROBLEMS OF IMPROPER STOCKING

Over Stocking

i   Competition amongst birds for food and water

ii Cannibalism

iii Uneven flock because stronger birds will get food and weaker ones will not

iv Bad litter

Under Stocking

i   Wastage of heat

ii More expenditure on gas, electricity, labour, etc.

TYPES OF FEEDING SYSTEMS

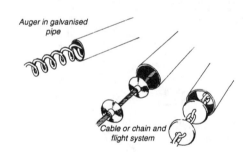

Auger in galvanised pipe

Cable or chain and flight system

i   Track and chain feeder system

ii   Cable and flight feeder system

iii Trough feeder

iv   Hopper feeder

v   Auger feeder

Track And Chain Feeder System

In this system the chain is in the side of the track that runs round the shed. As the track passes under a food bin, the chain collects food and moves it along. In this manner the entire feeder track is filled. This type of feeder system can be used in cage systems as well.

Cable And Flight, Auger Feeding System

This is another system in which either cable and flight or an auger runs inside a galvanized pipe. There are feed outlets (holes) in the pipe at regular intervals

Cable and flight or the auger brings the food from the bin and drops it off at the first outlet. When that outlet is full it will take the food to the next outlet. This process continues until all feed pans are filled.

Trough Feeders

These types of feeders are common with true battery cage systems.

A trough runs along the cages continuously from one end to the other, being filled from a hopper which runs on rails above the cages. As it moves along food is deposited in the trough. More modern troughs will have an auger or cable and flight system inside the trough to deliver the food.

Hopper Feeders

These are generally used in free range egg production systems and are manually filled. They vary in shape and size.

They are made in plastic or with galvanized metal. Since the development of automated systems these feeders have not been widely used.

Plastic hoppers are usually suspended from the roof inside a house. The galvanized hopper feeders are placed outside. They have the added advantage of a closeable lid which prevents any water getting into the food when not in use at night.

When selecting a type of feeder, consideration should be given to its design in respect of food wastage. If birds can flick food or too much is delivered in the trough it is wasted; 5 grams/day might go unnoticed but it amounts to 32p/bird/year.

Various devices are available for fitting to existing feeding systems to prevent wastage by over provision of food or birds flicking it onto the floor.

INTRODUCTION

Any livestock kept in intensive situations are prone to a whole range of diseases and other health disorders. The manager has to prevent ill health within the flock through careful routine hygiene, as well as attention to proper stocking, feeding and supervision.

The diagram that follows summarises these :

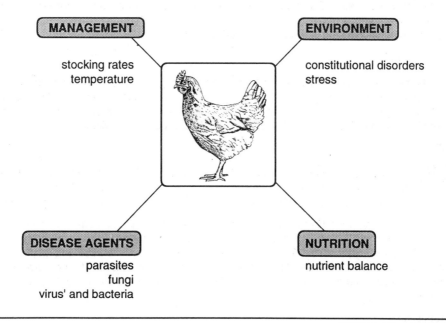

MANAGEMENT

stocking rates
temperature

ENVIRONMENT

constitutional disorders
stress

DISEASE AGENTS

parasites
fungi
virus' and bacteria

NUTRITION

nutrient balance

DISEASE AGENTS

External Parasites

The economic loss resulting from external parasites of poultry can be considerable. Although no sick or dying birds may be obvious, the gradual deterioration in the health of the flock, reduction in egg yield and impaired growth rate, can convert a reasonable profit into a considerable loss. For advice on treating parasites see your local poultry vet.

The most common of the external parasites are **lice and mites**. There are many types of these. Lice and their eggs can be seen when closely examining the fowls' feathers. The most common of the mite family are Red Mite and Northern Mite. These usually come out at night and take to the body of the fowl, especially the vent. They are bloodsuckers and usually live in cracks of nest boxes or underneath cage ledges.

I.B. (Infectious Bronchitis)

This is a viral infection. The virus can be transmitted from bird to bird through an airborne route, e.g. carried on dust particles. The virus can also be airborne between poultry houses and even from farm to farm through the ventilation system.

In younger birds I.B. can cause high mortality. In older birds I.B. does not cause mortality but does cause respiratory signs which include gurgling and wheezing. Egg production will decrease dramatically, sometimes to zero, and will never return to normal levels; deformed eggs with wrinkled shells will often be laid. There is no treatment for I.B., prevention by vaccination is the best method of control.

Egg Peritonitis

Inflamed peritoneum of ovaries in body cavity can be brought on. This also is similar to egg peristalis when egg goes backwards up oviduct, comes back down collecting double shell and egg white. This can be due to housing and environmental disorders or an after effect of Infectious Bronchitis. Consult your local poultry vet for advice.

N.D. (Newcastle Disease)

This disease is caused by a virus and is a **notifiable** disease. It is highly contagious through infected droppings and respiratory discharge between birds. Spread between farms is by infected equipment, trucks, personnel, wild birds or air.

The incubation period is usually between 3 to 6 days. Most commonly chickens and turkeys are affected by the disease. N.D. causes high mortality with depression and death in 3 to 5 days as major signs. Affected birds do not always show nervous and respiratory signs. There is no treatment for N.D. The only control is by vaccination during the rearing period, (see vaccination programme). The Ministry of Agriculture and the police must be notified.

Salmonella

This is a bacterial disease it can infect any part of the bird; this too is a **notifiable** disease There are several Salmonella: *Salmonella Pullorum, S. Enteritidis* and *S. Typhimurium.*

Pullorum

You can notice signs of B.W.D. (bacillary white diarrhoea), sick chicks, dying and huddled chicks. Birds recovering from the disease are carriers, and Salmonella can still be found in the droppings and nests. It can be carried through breeder hens to chicks, resulting in high mortality and all chicks being carriers.

Typhimurium and *Enteritidis*

These represent the 2 most important Salmonella. All laying stock and replacements must be tested for Salmonella by an independent laboratory by submitting carcasses, eggs, blood samples, cloacal swabs, and composite faecal samples on a regular basis.

Under the Testing and Registration Order of 1989, if a farmer wishes to sell eggs for human consumption he is required to;

i   register flocks of 100 or more birds

ii   monitor the flock for the presence of salmonellae by taking either composite faecal samples, cloacal swabs, dead birds, chicken box liners etc.,

The results are forwarded to M.A.F.F., and positive results may result in the slaughter of the flock.

The samples to be submitted are as follows:

Age	Sample
1-4 days	any dead on arrival (up to a maximum of 60). Chicken box liners (up to a maximum of 10)
4 days- 14 weeks	composite faecal sample or cloacal swabs
15-26 weeks	composite faecal sample or cloacal swabs
Every 12 weeks until slaughter	composite faecal sample or cloacal swabs

The composite faecal sample is made up of 1 gram samples taken from around the house, the number depending on the size of the flock. Assuming the flock is over 500 birds a 60 gram sample is required or 60 cloacal swabs.

Gumboro Disease (Infectious Bursal Disease)

This is a very important virus infection present in the UK since 1962. The symptoms are rather indefinite but show up most strongly in young chicks - especially broilers - followed by deaths. After this a large number of birds appear normal but are stunted in their growth and very unproductive.

Signs are anorexia, depression, huddling, ruffled feathers, vent pecking, diarrhoea and trembling. The cost of loss is not so much the death of chicks (5%) but the reduced performance of the survivors.

Marek's Disease

This disease causes tumours through the action of cell-associated herpes virus. It is possibly the most common of poultry diseases causing high mortality of 30% or more (for acute Marek's) in chickens aged 12 to 24 weeks. However, control through vaccination is now very successful. There is otherwise no treatment for the disease once contracted.

HOUSING/ENVIRONMENT DISORDERS

Good rearing techniques will minimise production stress. Follow breeders' management guide step by step during the rearing period and adjust these for local conditions if necessary.

Bird Requirements

Light:

Light is a vital tool in controlling the age of maturity of the birds during their early growth. Controlling the amount of light ensures that the birds reach the target weight before they start laying. Lighting conditions are easy to achieve in a controlled environment house. If an extensive system is used, then supplementary lighting will be required. Managers should use a standard lighting programme:

i   never increase light or intensity during the rearing period
ii   never decrease light or intensity during the laying period

Birds that lay too early due to incorrect lighting (increased too early) may suffer a prolapse in which case they are culled instantly.

Food

Flock weight unevenness will affect egg production. During the rearing period keep weighing the flock once per week and record, feed the birds accordingly and bring to correct weight at the point of lay. A small bird with a small body frame will struggle to lay eggs.

NUTRITIONAL DISORDERS

Having no access to soil or green plants and without any sunlight requires that layers food contains ample supplies of basic and essential trace elements. For this reason it is essential to use the proprietary feeds available.

In laying birds, vitamin D3 deficiency causes soft-shelled eggs and a drop in production. Maintain the correct ration suitable for the flock, e.g. Hybrid layers mash (17/18% protein).

OUTSIDER'S GUIDE

ROUTINE HEALTH MANAGEMENT

- ☛ To minimise disease, provide a water dip and disinfectant dip.

- ☛ Before restocking the house, make sure all equipment has been cleaned and disinfected thoroughly.

- ☛ Stick to the welfare code regarding stocking birds at the correct density (See Housing).

- ☛ Check equipment is working properly before putting into use. Allow no sharp or ridged corners to be exposed on which birds can hurt themselves.

- ☛ Make sure birds have had the full vaccination programme during the rearing period. Keep accurate recordings of these vaccinations.

- ☛ Provide goggles and rubber gloves in the house for use with disinfectants.

- ☛ Keep a fire extinguisher at hand, and keep it regularly serviced.

GENERAL VACCINATION PROGRAMME

A typical standard vaccination programme is shown below, although this varies with every company. Check, before starting the programme with the breeder's manual.

1 day old	@ hatchery, M.D.	vaccine inject 0.2 ml
1 day old	N.D. I.B.	course spray (half strength)
2 weeks old	Gumboro	
3	Gumboro	in drinking water
4	Gumboro	
5	I.B. & N.D.	in drinking water
10	I.B. & N.D	
12	E.T.	
16	I.B.	injected (0.5ml)

HEALTH

M.D.	Marek's disease
I.B.	Infectious Bronchitis
E.T.	Epidemic Tremour, also known as Avian Encephalomyelitis
N.D.	Newcastle disease

Giving Vaccinations

Read all instructions when using vaccines. Freeze dried vaccines should be opened under water. Follow up vaccines with a blood test, usually 3 weeks later.

Always precede dead injectable vaccines with live ones which give a quick but short lived response. Dead vaccines give a slow long lived response. Dead vaccines are oil based and are given by injection. Live vaccines are freeze-dried and are put in the drinking water or sprayed onto the birds.

When using vaccines, check storage requirements, expiry dates, dosage / 1000 birds, and keep vaccine batch number in case the vaccine does not seem to work.

LIVESTOCK TRANSPORTATION

Transporting should be carried out quietly and confidently, avoiding unnecessary struggling which could bruise or otherwise injure the birds. Adequate ventilation must be provided at all times. Birds should be protected from extremes of weather and should not be left for long periods during transportation.

INTRODUCTION

Poultry housing for layers has to be efficiently designed if the flock is to produce a profit margin worth the investment in labour and capital. Housing has to accommodate and facilitate the management of four elements:

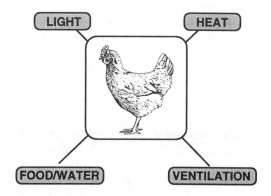

A deficiency in any one of these environmental conditions will reduce production from the layers. There are three main types of housing systems which attempt to cater for these environmental conditions:

cages	80%
alternative systems	20%

"Intensive systems" refers to those where a large number of birds are confined in a relatively small area. "Extensive systems" refers to those housing systems where small numbers of birds utilise relatively large areas of land.

Barn Eggs Production

Barn egg production is becoming increasingly popular. Essentially it is an intensive system with slatted and tiered areas of the house. Perches are incorporated into the house and the birds fill the whole volume of the building rather than just the floor area.

Stocking densities of up to 25 birds/m² are possible, making it comparable with the battery system, but more acceptable to some people as the birds have more freedom.

HOUSING

Deep Litter System

As the name implies the birds are placed on litter, usually woodshavings or chopped straw, which remains in the house for the duration of the flock. The stocking density is low, the maximum level being 17.1 kg/m². There are some husbandry problems associated with lice and other environmental conditions and production levels are lower than more intensive systems.

Some inputs are higher than battery systems (i.e. food and labour), making the system less efficient. Eggs from this system could be sold as Barn eggs which should command a premium price. However, the premium rarely covers the increased costs.

There are other variations on the deep litter system such as the aviary and the perchery, but these have the same inherent faults as true litter, although the stocking densities may be slightly higher.

Free range

By definition the birds have unrestricted access to pasture from which they can obtain some of their diet. They should be stocked at no more than 1000 birds/ha. Perches should be provided in the houses to enable all birds to roost off the floor.

Although given access to the outside, many birds never leave the confines of the building. Unfortunately with the current demand for free range eggs and the premium prices offered, many commercial units have been set up and do not conform with traditional free range philosophy, housing 1000s of birds on smaller areas.

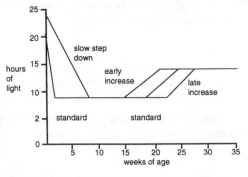

Costs are increased over battery and deep litter but there is a definite demand for free range eggs with a resultant premium being paid to producers.

Laying Cages - Battery

Most commercial layers (80%) are kept in this way. Its popularity is due to its higher bird performance, and lower labour costs compared with other systems. Different systems use steel and welded wire or timber and wire netting in horizontal, stepped or vertical configurations with 1 to 6 tiers. The most popular systems keep 3 to 5 birds per cage.

LIGHTING

Of all the environmental factors which require careful management, lighting is perhaps the most interesting as it has such an effect upon the performance of the laying hens.

Intensive systems have an environment where light is under direct management control. The diagram shows possible lighting regimes.

In all lighting systems provision should be made for a period of darkness in each 24 hour cycle. Where birds do not have access to daylight they should be given at least 8 hours lighting per day.

0 to 18 weeks (rearing):

to stimulate 'Autumn' natural light conditions, constant and fairly short day lengths should be created of about 8 hours (or decreasing to 8 hours). This is in order that the bird may develop properly and grow big enough to lay productively.

18 weeks onwards (laying):

in nature, the reproductive egg laying organ is stimulated by increasing amounts of light as would happen in the Spring. Thus in modern systems day length is increased to stimulate egg production. Light intensity therefore is kept greater than that during rearing. The only exception is during the first days of the chick's life when a strong light is required to help it find its way around and to get it off to a good start.

HOUSING REGULATIONS

Stocking Densities

System	Density (liveweight in relation to floor area)	Qualifications
Cages		
Birds being reared for laying	250 cm²/kg	For birds between 1 and 2 kg liveweight
Adult laying birds	These are subject to legal minimum requirements	
Deep litter	17kg/m²	
Birds being reared for laying		
Adult laying birds	17kg/m²	No more than 7 birds/m²
Table chickens	34kg/m²	
Straw yards		
Birds being reared for laying	10kg/m²	
Adult laying birds	8kg/m²	No more than 3 birds/m²
Housing for free range birds	As for deep litter systems	

Source: Codes of Recommendation for the Welfare of Livestock- (Domestic Fowls).

HOUSING

WASTE DISPOSAL

Manure has to be disposed of in the proper manner and stored at least 1 mile from the farm to prevent the chance of recurrence of disease within the house. Ammonia levels inside the house have to be monitored and therefore adequate ventilation is important to prevent high levels.

KEY POINTS - ENVIRONMENT

i   In a controlled environment the optimum temperature needs to be about 21°C

ii   The birds have to have access to clean water and food at all times

iii   Enough light should be available so that all the birds can be seen clearly when being inspected; about 10 Lux

iv   All equipment should be constructed and maintained in such a way as to avoid subjecting the birds to excessive noise or allowing them to injure or harm themselves

Requirements For Caged Birds

Item	Specification
Trough space per bird	4 cm
Drinker space	2 nipples per cage.
Cage space	450 cm² per bird minimum, with three or more birds per cage
Light	10 Lux

Current proposals are for a minimum of 600 cm²/bird making it a less efficient system. In the future **cage** systems may be outlawed altogether as has happened in some European countries.

Laying hens do not have a reproductive phase in the sense that other livestock enterprises have. Layers are hybrids and so there is no point in breeding from them. Layers exist solely to produce eggs as efficiently as possible over their lifetime.

REPRODUCTION

However, two aspects need to be attended to that lie within the management scope of an egg producer. The first is the brooding (rearing) of chicks up to the point of lay, and the second is the production of the egg which is normally a reproductive activity.

KEY FACTS FOR BROODING

This is the period when young chicks in the first few weeks of their lives require extra protection and heat.

Using Cages - Requirements 0-6 Weeks

Space:

Floor space	180 cm²/bird
Feeder space	2.5 cm/bird
Drinker space	2.5 cm/bird
1 nipple but access to 2	15 birds

Allow 25% more area per bird when hot conditions and marginal ventilation are present. Use paper over the wire floor for the first 10 days, ensure it extends under all drinkers to give chicks easy access to water.

Temperature

Pre-heat house for 24 hours and maintain temperature of **29-32°C** at cage level. Reduce temperature by about 4°C per week, aim for 20°C at 21 days. However, use chicks as a guide as these figures can vary; contented chirruping chicks evenly spread throughout the area indicates that conditions are right. Cold chicks will huddle together and hot chicks will pant and be listless.

Feed

A chick starter crumb should be used, it should contain **19-20 % protein**. Initially it should be placed on paper or trays and fed for the **first 6 weeks** or until target weight for age is reached. Insoluble grit such as granite or flint should also be fed with feed to aid digestion.

Lighting

The lighting programme begins at day one and must be co-ordinated throughout the life of the flock.

REPRODUCTION

Water

This is provided in cups or nipples with a **maximum of 10 birds/cup** or nipple and a minimum of 2 cups or nipples/cage.

Humidity and ventilation

Maintain a minimum relative **humidity of 50%** for first 6 weeks to promote good feathering.

Ventilation must perform 5 functions:

i	provide fresh air
ii	remove stale air
iii	control temperature
iv	control humidity
v	remove dust

Floor Brooding - Requirements From 0 - 6 Weeks

Floor space	18/m²
Feeder space	2.5cm
Drinker space	2.5cm
1 nipple or cup	20 birds

Litter

A non-toxic, friable litter such as wood **shavings** should be used at a depth of **8 cm**.

Temperature

Pre-heat house 24 hours prior to chick arrival. Operate brooders so a temperature of **32°C** is maintained **5cm above the litter** at the edge of the canopy. Reduce temperature by 4°C per week to around 20°C at 21 days. However, as with cage brooding, use the chicks as a guide.

Feed, light , humidity and ventilation are the same as for cage brooding. Water is provided by 8-10 bell drinkers/1000 birds. Supplementary feeders should be available if necessary.

GROWING PERIOD 6-17 WEEKS

Key Records

i	body weight	ii	feed intake
iii	water intake	iv	hours of light
v	temperature		
vi	health		

Vaccination: Infectious Bronchitis, vaccinations vary according to disease history of site, risk of infection, etc. , and to cover such diseases as Newcastle disease, Gumboro, Epidemic Tremours. Veterinary advice should be taken.

Mortality

Pullets body weights can be checked regularly, beginning at 4 weeks of age. Uniformity should also be checked, 80% of flock should be within ± 10% of average weight. Breeding companies provide information on their stock body weight.

Space Requirements

	Cages	Litter
Floor space	400cm²	9/m²
Feeder space	5.0 cm	7.5 cm
Drinker space	5.0 cm	5.0 cm
Cups or nipples	Maximum of 10 birds/cup or nipple	
	Minimum of 2 cups or nipples/cage	

Ration

At **6 weeks** of age the ration should be **changed to a growers** ration. But if body weights are below target, the starter ration can be continued until target weight for that age is achieved. Ad lib feeding can be done over the two periods or feed restricted during the 6-17 week period if weight problems occur.

Disease Control

Where possible an all-in-all-out system should be used. Essential visitors only should be allowed on site, and other hygiene precautions should be taken such as foot dips.

REPRODUCTION

Coccidiosis is a protozoal disease of the gut, it can be prevented by good hygiene and additives in feed during the period of 0-17 weeks. Food containing an Anti-Coccidial Supplement has this declared on the feed delivery ticket ('A.C.S.').

Beak Trimming

This should be done around 5-8 days of age if desired.

Lighting

During the brooding and growing period the day length is gradually reduced to 8 hours over a period of two weeks. In addition the light intensity is reduced to dim, around 1-2 Lux. This light length and intensity is maintained until 18 weeks of age, after which time it is increased gradually to 15/16 hours/day and held throughout the laying period, (14 hours day length should be reached by the peak production at 28 weeks).

LAYING PERIOD

The laying period starts from about 20 weeks of age until about 72 weeks at which point it is no longer economic to maintain the birds and they are culled. During this period egg production climbs rapidly to a peak of about 95% at 28 weeks, and then declines to about 60% to 65% at 72 weeks.

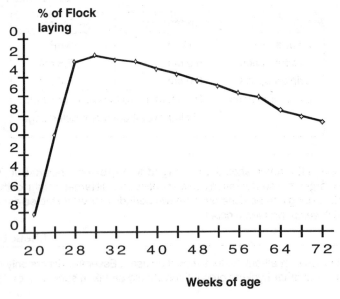

PHYSICAL PERFORMANCE

KEY ASSESSMENT QUESTIONS

Hen housed egg Nº to 76 weeks*	**295**
Hen day egg Nº to 76 weeks**	305
Age at sexual maturity	19 - 20 weeks
Age at peak production	29 weeks
Peak production	95%
Average egg weight	63g
Livability 0 to 20 weeks	97%
Livability 21 to 76 weeks	93%
Feed consumed per dozen eggs	1.8 to 2.0 kg
Daily feed consumption	120g
End of lay carcass weight	2.00kg

   ***Hen housed egg numbers** is the figure derived from the total number of eggs produced by a flock divided by the number of birds in the flock at the onset of lay. Since it takes into account the rate of lay and the mortality it is an very good indicator of relative profitability. The target for well managed flocks should exceed 280 eggs per hen housed.

   ****Hen day egg numbers** are the average number of eggs produced over a period of time by the number of hens alive during that period and thus ignores the effects of mortality.

GROSS MARGINS

   The figures following are for different systems of production. The margin achieved under each system is always dependent upon the skill of management, and to a small extent, the breed used.

OUTSIDER'S GUIDE

PERFORMANCE

GROSS MARGINS

Battery Egg Production (Brown Eggs)

OUTPUT PER HEN		£
Eggs	278 (23.2 doz.) in 52 weeks @ 45p/doz.	10.43
Less	depreciation	2.20
	mortality	0.13
TOTAL		**8.10**
Variable costs		
	concentrates 44kg @ 16.5p/kg	6.58
	electricity	0.35
	variable sundries;	
	(vet, medicines, water, insurance, repairs)	0.38
TOTAL		**7.81**

Gross margin/hen housed (in pence)	**79**
Gross margin/dozen eggs (in pence)	**3.4**

Source: ABC

Price assumes eggs are sold straight to packer. There are stil contracts available for "barn" type eggs and a premium price is paid but this is being eroded as supply has exceeded demand and, as with Free Range, only applies to the large grades of eggs.

NOTES:

Depreciation:	point of lay pullet (18-20) weeks old) valued at £2.60 minus cull/casualty hen price of 25p gives charge of £2.35
Labour:	about £1.18 to £1.19 /hen
Dead stock depreciation: approximately £1.18- £1.19p/hen	
To break even a selling price of 53.3p per dozen eggs must be obtained if deadstock depreciation is included if not the price must be 49.8p.	

PERFORMANCE

Deep Litter Egg Production (Barn Eggs)

	OUTPUT PER HEN	£
Eggs	270 (22.5 dozen) in 52 weeks @ 54p/doz.	12.15
Less	Depreciation	2.20
	Mortality	0.21
TOTAL		**9.74**
Variable costs		
	concentrates 47kg @ 15.6p/kg	7.33
	electricity	0.32
	variable sundries;	
	(vet, medicines, water, insurance, repairs)	0.35
TOTAL		**8.00**

Gross margin/hen (in pence)	**174**
Gross margin/dozen eggs (in pence)	**7.72**

Labour £2.00 - £2.05/hen. Deadstock depreciation approx. £1.35/hen.

There are still contracts available for "barn" type eggs and a premium price is paid but this is being eroded as supply has exceeded demand and as with Free Range only applies to the large grades of eggs.

PERFORMANCE

Free Range Egg Production (Brown Eggs)

	OUTPUT PER HEN	£
Eggs	270 (22.5 dozen) in 52 weeks @ 64p/dozen	14.40
Less	depreciation	2.20
	mortality; 12% of £2.50 pullet	0.21
TOTAL		**11.99**
Variable Costs		
	concentrates 48kg @ 16.2p/kg	8.16
	electricity	0.31
	variable sundries,	
	(vet, medicines, water, insurance, repairs)	0.35
TOTAL		**8.82**

Gross margin/hen place (£)	**3.77**
Gross margin/dozen eggs (in pence)	**16.75**

Producer Returns And Cost Of Production

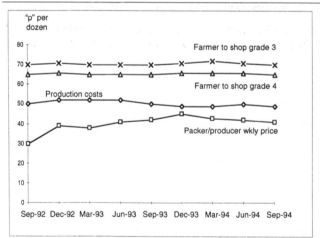

The gross margin will vary from year to year depending on the egg price (supply/demand). In addition margins may also vary according to the feed price and the cost of point of lay pullets.

OUTSIDER'S GUIDE

FIXED COSTS

Profitable farms manage to **minimise fixed costs**, and to **maximise output** from their type of farming system so that fixed costs per unit output are as low as possible.

The figures below are typical levels of fixed costs for arable farms with pigs and poultry. Individual farms will vary in their levels of fixed costs for specific reasons - e.g. new farms will have high **rental charges of 40% to 70%** higher than those quoted. **Larger farms** will tend to have lower costs/hectare.

Farm type	TOTAL FIXED COSTS (£/ha)		
	<100 ha	100 - 200 ha	>200 ha
Arable farms with pigs and poultry and > 25% gross output from pigs or poultry	1310	1085	760

Source: A.B.C.

Fixed Cost Elements

*The table below shows the components of these fixed costs:

Item - Arable with Pigs / Poultry	£/ha
Regular labour	430
Depreciation	95
Repairs, tax and insurance - equipment	98
Fuel and electricity	80
Contract charges - hedging/ditching	33
Land maintenance (fencing, repairs etc.).	48
Rent & rates	155
Fees, office expenses	75
TOTAL	**1113**

PERFORMANCE

THE
OUTSIDER'S GUIDE
to
INDOOR PIGS

1995 Edition

The domesticated pig has been derived mainly, and in varying proportions, from the European species *SUS SCROFA*, and *SUS VITATUS* the pot-bellied, small, black pig of sub-tropical and tropical S.E. Asia.

The pig is a very versatile animal and is kept under varying climatic conditions; in small herds kept outdoors owned by peasant farmers and in large intensive indoor units. The diet may consist of grass, forages, roots or cereals and highly digestible proteins. Generally in the Western world pigs are kept intensively, while in the rest of the world they are kept as foragers or scavengers eating cheap, by-product type foods.

THE WORLD

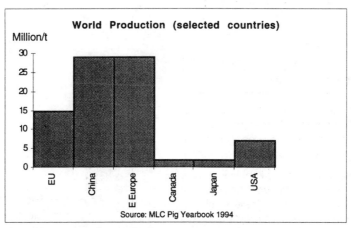

World Production (selected countries)

Source: MLC Pig Yearbook 1994

The pig is the main source of meat for human consumption.

World Production Of Meat

	'000 m/tonnes	%
Pigs	72571	41
Cattle types	53293	29
Poultry	43046	24
Sheep/goats	9902	6
Total	**178812**	**100**

Source: F.A.O.

PRODUCTION

Production And Consumption

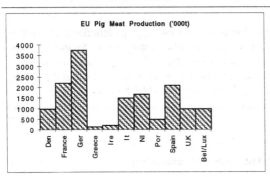

EU Pig Meat Production ('000t)

Source: MLC Pig Yearbook 1994

In the EU during the last few years consumption of pigmeat per head of the population has increased from 40 kg to 41kg/head/year. Production in the EU over the same period has stayed the virtually the same.

THE UNITED KINGDOM

It is estimated that there are about 12,000 pig herds in the UK. Over recent years the breeding herd has been concentrated in fewer but larger herds (approximately 3,500).

The majority of pigs are kept in intensive units with high capital investment in specialist buildings and equipment. There is now a small but increasing % of pigs kept in low cost outdoor units for which it is important to choose the right breed for the climate and the right stocking density for the soil type. Given this and good husbandry, results can approach those of indoor intensive units.

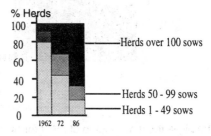

Source: Pig Improvement Company

Consumption

Consumption has slightly increased in the last year to about 21.2kg per head up from 20kg, with pork consumption increasing at the expense of bacon and ham.

Production

Currently the UK is 75% self-sufficient in pork and so this country is an importer. However, being only 35% self-sufficient in bacon and ham, 27% of bacon supplies come from Denmark and 22% from the Netherlands.

OUTSIDER'S GUIDE

UK Annual Pigmeat Consumption Per Head (kg)

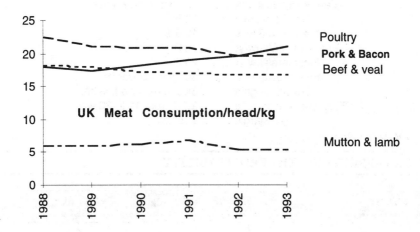

The Pig Cycle

Pigs reach puberty at 6 months and have a short pregnancy of four months and are very prolific (10 reared per litter). This means that the size of the breeding herd and therefore the number of slaughter pigs can vary considerably from one year to the next.

There is virtually no price support mechanism in the UK and thus with a static demand for pigmeat (unlike in the EU 12) any over supply will have a big effect on price. Any high price triggers expansion and the market becomes rapidly over supplied and prices drop.

Monthly Average All Pig Price (A.A.P.P.) /kg Deadweight

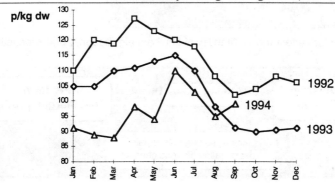

PRODUCTION

KEY ASSESSMENT QUESTIONS

Farrowing ing index .... 2.25 litters/sow/year
Pigs born alive 12.5
Mortality to 3 wks 12.5%
Pigs weaned/sow/yr 23.2
Finishers/sow/yr 20.2
Target growth rate .... 80 kg in 20 weeks
Liveweight gain .... 6kg/week for a finisher
Food conversion ratio .... 2.7:1 from 11 to 20 weeks
Gross Margin £351.37

Source: M.L.C. Pig Yearbook '94

FACTORS AFFECTING SOW PROFITABILITY

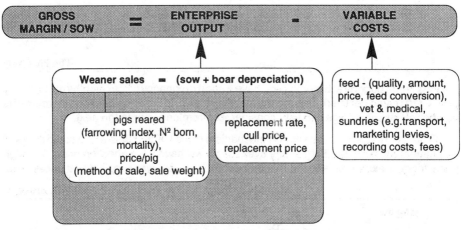

Note: similar factors affect the profitability of finishers pig (bacon, pork) production.

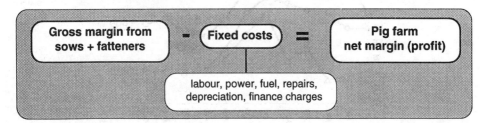

OUTSIDER'S GUIDE

THE PRODUCTION CYCLE

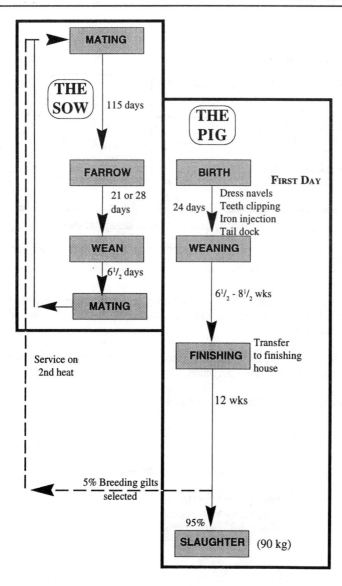

MARKETING

PRODUCTS

Traditional Products

Porkers (60 - 75kg) fresh pigmeat

Baconers (90kg) cured product

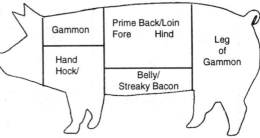

The trend now is for the majority of producers to sell by deadweight, and the abattoir/processor decides which carcasses or parts of the carcasses go for fresh pigmeat and which will go for curing as bacon.

Weaners - some producers sell 25-30kg pigs, bought by feeding herds who grow them on to slaughter weight.

MARKET OUTLETS

i   Finished pigs can be sold either through a marketing organization or co-operative where transport and abattoir arrangements are usually made by the group manager usually on a deadweight basis.

ii Direct to an abattoir. This may be on an annual contract or on a weekly price basis. This is called selling on a **deadweight** basis.

iii Auction. **Liveweight** basis and accounts for less than 10% of pigs sold.

Male Pigs

Most male pigs are sold entire (not castrated) with advantages of:

> **faster growth rate**
> **food conversion ratio**
> **improved gradings**

MARKETING

MARKET INFORMATION

Carcass Information

The M.LC., acting as an independent organisation, classify (i.e. grade) about 80% of all clean pig carcasses and young boar carcasses weighing up to 62Kg.

Carcasses are **dressed** to the agreed specification (liveweight minus specific offals) and the following measurement/assessments are made upon which abattoirs base their grade and price:

M.L.C. Grading

> **cold carcass weight**
> **backfat thickness (usually P_2 or P_1 & P_3)**
> **visible carcass faults**
> **length (optional)**
> **conformation (optional)**

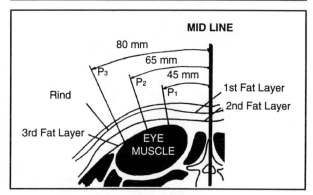

Abattoirs And Prices

There are about 700 abattoirs in Great Britain which are involved in slaughtering pigs; of these 60 are specialist pig abattoirs.

There is no direct price support mechanism/subsidy for UK producers. Abattoirs determine their own prices for the respective grades/carcass weight and these are usually related to the weekly average all pigs price (A.A.P.P.). The **A.A.P.P.** is published each week in the farming press and fluctuates according to supply and demand.

MARKETING

The A.A.P.P. 1990-94 (pence/kg dw)

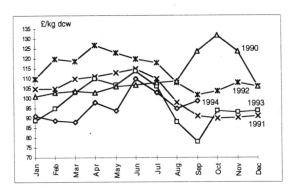

Weights, Prices & Gradings (P$_2$)

Lwt	KO%	D wt	Grades (mm - P$_2$- fat)				
kg	%	kg	first	second	third	fourth	fifth
55 to 68	72	40.5 to 50	7-11	13	15	17	17+
Price	=	A.A.P.P.	+11p	+9p	+7p	+3p	-1p
68 to 80	74	50.5 to 60	7-12	14	16	18	18+
Price	=	A.A.P.P.	+7p	+5p	+3p	-1p	-5p
80 to 85	75	60.5 to 63	7-12	14	16	18	
Price	=	A.A.P.P.	+4p	+2p	-1p	-7p	
85 to 98	76	63.5 to 75	7-14	15	17	19+	
Price	=	A.A.P.P.	0	-2p	-5p	-13p	

Levies

All slaughter pigs carry a levy of approximately £1.21/pig which is collected by M.L.C. for promotion and a general levy (R+D). Carcass classification is calculated on a local basis.

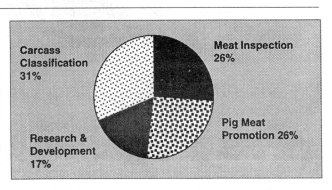

MARKETING

EU Regulations

A pig carcass grading scheme was introduced in January 1989 to cover all pigs slaughtered within the EU.

The basis of this scheme is lean meat content. At present, until abattoirs acquire new measuring equipment this will be calculated from the fat measurement of the carcass in relation to its weight and there will be no compulsion on the abattoirs to pay for carcasses on a % lean meat basis.

The New Grading Regime (Definitions Of Conformation & Fatness)

Grade		% lean meat
S		>60
E	Excellent	55-60
U	Very good	50-55
R	Good	45-50
O	Fair	40-45
P	Poor	< 40

Simple ready-reckoner tables are available which convert P_2 thickness and liveweight into % lean meat.

BREEDS & SYSTEMS

INTRODUCTION

Breeding stock needs to be capable of producing **large numbers of pigs** with **quick** and **efficient growth** into **lean carcasses**.

Breed Improvement

Currently the leading breeding companies are maintaining two lines ('male' and 'female') within each breed population in order to maximise the rate of genetic improvement. One line is used to produce males where selection is made on growth efficiency and leaness, whilst the other line is used to produce females where selection is based on prolificacy and mothering ability.

DAM LINES

SIRE LINES

NEW
F_1 PARENT GILT

NEW BOAR

Boars and gilts with high levels of performance in these traits are given high indices; however, each breeding company operates a different index range, thus pigs from one company cannot be compared with pigs from another.

Main Breeds

CHARACTERISTICS			ECONOMIC STRENGTHS/WEAKNESSES					
Breed	**Coat**	**Ears**	**P**	**M**	**H**	**GR**	**FCR**	**L**
L. White	White	pricked	+	av	+	+	+	av
Landrace	White	lop	+	av	av	+	+	av
Welsh	White	lop	+	av	av	+	+	av
Duroc	Ginger	lop	av	+	+	av	av	av
Hampshire	Black. White saddle	pricked	-	av	+	-	-	+
British	Black,							
Saddleback	Black. White saddle	lop	-	+	+	-	-	-
Pietrain	White. Black spots	lop	-	-	-	-	-	+
Key;	P=prolific; M=mothering ability; H=hardiness; GR=growth rate; FCR=food conversion ratio; L=lean; '+' indicates better than average.							

COMMERCIAL OBJECTIVES

Commercial producers require a first cross (F1) hybrid female. Maximum litter production is achieved (through hybrid vigour/heterosis) using these F1 females with either a pure bred or cross-bred terminal sire. Cross-bred terminal sires have a better reproductive performance and produce more lean meat in the carcasses of their progeny than pure-bred terminal sires. Pure bred terminal sires are also used.

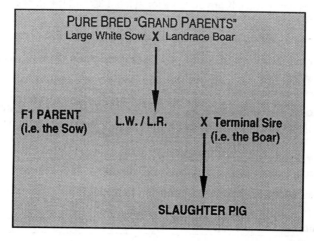

PURE BRED "GRAND PARENTS"
Large White Sow **X** Landrace Boar

F1 PARENT
(i.e. the Sow)   L.W. / L.R.   **X** Terminal Sire
(i.e. the Boar)

SLAUGHTER PIG

On-Farm Policy

Flying herd policy

The herd consists entirely of F1 hybrid females purchased from breeding companies or private breeders. New stock should be isolated and then integrated into the herd to prevent health risks to the existing herd and/or the new stock.

D.I.Y. Policy

The herd contains a small section of sows (purchased or home bred through A.I.) and these produce the F1 hybrids from which the slaughter pigs are produced, i.e. Large white grandparent sows inseminated with Landrace semen to produce the F1 LW/LR hybrid gilt. Terminal sires need to be unrelated and are usually bought-in.

BREEDS & SYSTEMS

OUTDOOR PIGS

Currently, outdoor pig systems are used for **weaner production from breeding sows**. Weaners then are transferred to conventional indoor systems.

However, outdoor systems are now being used for the follow on (feeding) stages, and some outdoor systems take pig production right through to finishing stages.

Estimates suggest that between 20% and 25 % of breeding sows are housed outdoors and that conditions in the UK are suitable for at least 30% of the total pig production to be produced outdoors.

The reasons for the growth in interest are as follows:

i   lower capital cost per breeding sow and fixed costs dramatically reduced in total by 50%

ii   low maintenance costs

iii   improved husbandry techniques, regular farrowing and earlier weaning now give pig managers results comparable with those obtained in much more expensive indoor accommodation (refer to 🐷)

iv   lower break-even point is possible with good management

v   improved public image regarding pig welfare

vi   potential for free-range price premium (reducing)

Requirements For Outdoor Pig Production

Breed   Incorporation of Duroc and Hampshire breeds give hardiness. Most commercial breeding companies sell crosses specifically for the outdoor market.

Soils   Free draining

Climate   Low rainfall - avoid excessively wet areas

Housing   Movable, no floor structures, (well insulated for follow-on weaners and provide ample bedding)

Labour   Dedicated and motivated staff essential.

NUTRITION

FEEDING PIGS

Pigs are one-stomach animals able to utilise a wide range of foods. In the UK, **hybrid pigs** are usually **fed high energy cereal** diets balanced with supplementary protein, minerals and vitamins.

Main feed constituents are wheat, barley, soyabean and other vegetable proteins. High value feeds are expensive representing over 80% of variable costs of production.

KEY ASSESSMENT QUESTIONS

Breeding	Av.	Top 10%
Average weaning age (days)	25	24
Sow feed/sow/year (t)	1.3	1.23
Feed/pig reared; Sow feed(kg)	67	55
Creep feed(kg)	0.3	0.3
Rearing (6 to 30 kg)		
Feed conversion ratio	1.79	1.52
Daily gain (g)	448	486
Feed/pig reared (Kg)	50.5	40.6
Feeding (30 kg to 85 kg)		
Feed conversion rate	2.60	2.34
Food/pig (kg)	163	138
Daily liveweight gain (g/day)	586	615

Source: M.L.C. Pig Year Book 1994

FEEDING AIMS

Breeding Stock

Maintain the breeding stock in a healthy and fit condition to achieve up to **2.4 - 2.5 production cycles** per annum on **three to four week weaning**.

NUTRITION

Gilts

At six months on average, gilts reach puberty or first heat. The best practice should be for **first mating to occur** at the **3rd heat** or 4th heat having being fed ad lib from selection/purchase up to this time so that they have a long and productive breeding life. Gilts should be a minimum of 210/220 days old and weigh 130/140kg at service to ensure maximum lifetime performance.

Sows

Pregnancy.

The first 3 or 4 weeks of pregnancy is critical for **maximum litter size**. It is essential that the sow has minimum stress and a maximum of 2.5 kg food/day during this period to ensure maximum implantation. In the last month increase feed intake by 50% to support full foetal growth.

Lactation.

Relatively high levels of energy feed intake (6 - 9 kg/day sow nuts) are required to maintain condition for the next breeding cycle.

Dry Period.

Following removal of the sucking stimulus the sow normally dries up and comes on heat 4-7 days later, when she is again mated. Main aim of this period is to maximize the **number of eggs** produced and aid recovery from any negative energy balance of lactation. Flushing (high energy intake) can help.

Sow Feeding Scales

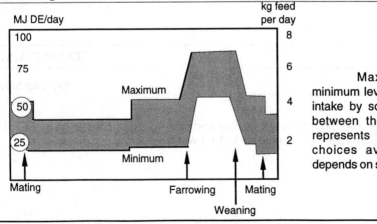

Maximum and minimum levels of energy intake by sow. The area between the two levels represents the range of choices available and depends on sow condition.

Boars

General aim is to keep them in a hard, fit lean condition. Overweight boars are lazy, slow to work and too heavy for smaller sows and gilts.Generally they need 4 or 5 days rest between sows to ensure maximum fertility.

FEEDING GROWING / FATTENING STOCK

Suckling Pigs

The **aim** is to maximize new born pigs' disease resistance. It is essential that they ingest as much **colostrum** as possible to obtain protective antibodies **within the first 6 hours**.

Have clean **water available** at all times to increase dry matter intake. Of all systems, **nipple/bite** systems are functional and almost impossible to foul.

Sweetening agents can be added to encourage intake. Creep feed if fed should be changed at least once a day to maintain freshness and encourage eating.

Growing And Finishing Pigs

The **AIM** is to produce finished pigs of slaughterable weight of top quality grade in the minimum of time with the minimum of food costs. It is important that enough **Lysine** is fed to avoid limiting pig growth. Many herds today are feeding ad lib right through to slaughter with growth rates and food conversion showing big improvements.

Feed needs are determined by sex, genotype, physical and social environment, and by stage of growth. A simple dual feed may be used ad lib, but with or without a restriction in the final weeks before slaughter (to avoid grading problems due to too much fat deposition as the pig gets older).

Factors Considered

Many factors determine finisher production - **feed ingredient price, product price (porker, cutter, baconer) feed levels and product turnover for different products** - so many producers use computers for linear program least cost rations, and simulation programs to optimise inputs and outputs.

NUTRITION

RECOMMENDED FEED LEVELS

 Typical Diet Specifications

Units	Dig. En/kg MJ	Oil %	Fibre %	Protein %	Lysine %	Cost/t £
Creep	17	9	1.5	22	1.6	560
Grower	14	4.5	3	20	1.2	190
Finisher	13.5	3	5	19	1	170
Sow	13.5	5	5	17	0.8	160

 Typical Feed Amounts

Units	Body Wt. kg	Energy MJ DE/day	Feed intake kg	Diet Type
Piglets	6	5	ad lib	Creep
Weaners	10	12	ad lib	Creep
Growers	20	18	ad lib	Grower
Finishers				
a)	50	26	ad lib/restrict	Finisher
b)	70	32	ad lib/restrict	Finisher
Dry sows	140	30	2.3	Sow
Lact. sows	140	90	2.3 + .45*	Sow
Gilts	90	35	ad lib	Sow
Boar	160	30	2.3	Sow

* + 0.45 kg per suckler.

INTRODUCTION

There are probably more diseases that affect pigs than any other species of farm livestock; in addition, many pig units are intensively designed thus facilitating the spread of any new disease; furthermore still many diseases are viral in origin and cannot be cured by antibiotic therapy.

Given the right conditions some bacteria can multiply at the rate of one/hour; thus after one hour, one bacterium has given rise to two.... and after 24 hrs one has given rise to over 8 million. The right conditions are warmth, moisture and food (dung, dirt, dust).

SOURCES OF DISEASE

There is no single disease which is of more concern to the pig manager than any other. The most important thing is **prevention**.

This means strict hygiene methods which apply to **EVERYONE GOING ONTO A PIG UNIT,** especially company representatives or anyone going from farm to farm.

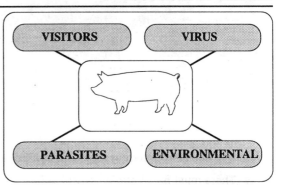

DISEASE PREVENTION

Herd Health Security

i Visitors   **do not enter unit without permission and:**

should be kept to minimum;
may need 24 hrs clearance from pigs;
wear units own boots/overalls;
use foot dips.

ii Transport   **food lorries should blow food to bins in from perimeter and:**

pig wagons should load up at perimeter;
knacker wagon should collect off-site;
misc. vehicles, if necessary, have wheel dip/spray.

IDEAL UNIT LAYOUT

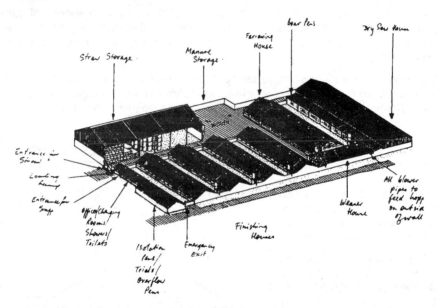

iii Replacement breeding stock require isolation.

iv There must be a vermin control policy.

Vaccination Programme

All vaccines should be stored at 3-8°C and generally, if a bottle is opened, it should be emptied.

i   Erysipelas

Erysipelas is caused by bacteria which can survive for years in organic matter. Does not always cause the classic purple, diamond marks on the skin. Responsible for abortions, arthritis and death through heart attacks. All breeding stock (including boars) should be vaccinated at least twice a year.

ii   S.M.E.D.I.

Caused by parvo-viruses which inhabit the uterus of gilts/sows and effect reproductive performance without causing the pig herself any illness. Results in stillbirths, mummified piglets, embryonic mortality (small litters) or infertility. All breeding stock, including boars, should undergo a routine vaccination programme.

iii   Other diseases

These may be prevented by a vaccination policy depending on specific problems/veterinary advice.

Miscellaneous Preventative Measures

i   Parasites

All breeding stock should be routinely treated for worms, lice and mange, usually twice a year with one of the many proprietary products available.

ii   Anaemia

All baby piglets should be given iron to prevent anaemia as the sows milk is naturally deficient in iron.

iii Routine vets visits

Very useful as an aid to preventing disease.

SOME NOTIFIABLE DISEASES

Anthrax

Very rare but is of bacterial origin and usually results in death.

Aujesky's Disease

A virus causing abortion in pregnant sows and scours together with high mortality rates in young pigs.

Foot and Mouth Disease

A virus causing blisters on the feet and tongue of cloven-footed animals.

Swine Fever

Highly contagious virus disease usually resulting in a high fever and death.

Swine Vesicular Disease

Virus causing very similar symptoms to Foot and Mouth Disease.

Porcine Respiratory Syndrome (PRRS) "Blue Ear"

Still birth, very high mortality in piglets, reduced finishing herd performance.

HEALTH

SOME COMMON DISEASES

Piglet Scours

Can be nutritional (usually yellow) but often is of bacterial or viral origin. The most common cause is a bacterium called E.coli, of which there are many strains.

Meningitis

Caused by a bacteria which can often be treated with penicillin if caught early enough. Usually associated with stress of weaning but other stresses include moving, mixing, temperature, low ventilation rates. Symptoms include unco-ordinated movement and then death.

Enzootic Pneumonia

Is an infection of the lungs caused by a virus. Leads to coughing, loss of condition and eventually perhaps death.

Atrophic Rhinitis

Deformation/destruction of the turbinate bones in the nostrils. Symptoms include twisted snouts, runny eyes and sneezing, and often leads to other secondary infections of the respiratory tract.

Swine Dysentery

A disease of growing/finishing pigs caused by a type of virus. It is easily spread in houses that have dung scraped along the length of the dung passageway. Symptoms are blood stained scouring.

Mastitis/Metritis/Agalactia (M.M.A.)

This is a post-farrowing disorder of sows. It is multi-factoral in origin, and often leads to a shortage of milk (hence piglet mortality) and sometimes subsequent infertility in the sows after weaning.

LEGAL ASPECTS

Code For The Use Of Medicines

i Source

Obtain products only from veterinary surgeons or registered agricultural merchants.

ii Storage

Temperature and light can be critical. Some products must be kept under lock/key.

iii Records

Must be kept for purchases and use (date, quantity, stock). In some cases empty bottles must be returned to supplier.

iv Withdrawal times

Withdrawal periods are laid down for specific products relating to the time between the end of the treatment and the date of slaughter. It is important to avoid certain residue in meat for human consumption.

Miscellaneous

Casualty pigs must be certified free from antibiotics, fit to travel, the carcass must be free from infection and suitable for human consumption as outlined in the new meat inspection regulations introduced in January 1991.

HEALTH

SYSTEMS

There is an extremely wide range and combination of housing systems.

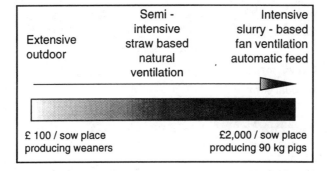

THE PIG ENVIRONMENT

On intensively designed units with high capital investment the aim has to be high output, and the indoor hybrid pig has to be provided with an environment (both climatic and social) which is conducive to maximum performance (ref).

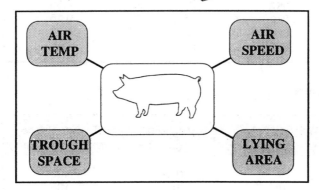

Specialist housing exists for all production stages providing the right environment and allowing quick and easy livestock movement when required.

HOUSING

KEY ASSESSMENT QUESTIONS

Climatic Environment

Production stage	Lower critical temperature °C		Max. air speed (m/sec)
	Straw	Slatted	
Service area			
Individual sows	15	18	0.2
Grouped sows	10	-	0.2
Pregnant sows			
Individual sows	19	22	0.2
Grouped sows	15	-	0.2
Lactating sows	19	22	0.15
Growing pigs			
Birth	28	30	0.1
5kg	27	30	0.1
7kg	22	26	0.15
10kg	20	25	0.15
15kg	18	22	0.15
20kg	15	19	0.15
30kg	13	17	0.25
90kg	11	15	0.3

Social Environment

Weight of pig (kg)	Lying area* (m²)	Trough Space (restrict feed -mm)
5	0.07	100
10	0.1	130
20	0.15	150
40	0.25	200
60	0.35	240
80	0.45	260
100	0.5	280
* Add at least 25% to lying area to give total area.		

OUTSIDER'S GUIDE

Waste Disposal

The amount of excreta produced by pigs varies considerably; best estimates are:-

Class of Pig	Excreta (dung + urine) litres/day
Pregnant sow	4.5
Lactating sow	15
Grower 20-90kg	
dry meal	4.0
liquid meal (2.5:1)	4.0
liquid meal (4:1)	7.0
swill/whey	14.0

Both slurry and farm yard manure (F.Y.M.) can be used to good effect to replace part or all of the fertilizer requirements of a wide range of crops.

Pollution

With slurry care should be taken to avoid pollution of the air (housing estates), water courses and underground water collection areas; furthermore the amount of slurry applied to land each year needs limiting especially to avoid copper toxicity to crops/other grazing livestock and also care should be taken to avoid structural damage to the soil.

LEGAL REQUIREMENTS

Planning (Town & Country General Development Order 1988)

Specific planning permission must be obtained where:

a) the ground area of new or extended building exceeds 465 m² . This figure includes any adjacent building work over the last 2 years

b) the height of any part of the building work exceeds 3m, and is within 3km of the perimeter of an aerodrome

c) the height of any part of the building work exceeds12m

d) any part of the work would be within 25m of a trunk/classified road

e) the construction is for the accommodation of livestock or the storage of slurry/sewage within 400m of certain "protected" buildings where people live or work. (The main farmhouse and farm workers cottages are outside the meaning of "protected" buildings.)

HOUSING

**Water Act 1989, Environmental Protection Act 1990,
Control of Pollution Regulations 1991**

Legislation which may effect the application of manures and other wastes (including afterbirths and dead pigs) is wide ranging and covered by several Acts of Parliament. The main provisions are:

i   direct discharge (or indirect seepage) of farm wastes to water courses is forbidden. Organic matter can cause de-oxygenation of water, resulting in death of fish/plants; disease organisms can be spread via water courses.

ii   pollution of ground waters should be avoided if water is abstracted for human consumption.

iii   atmospheric pollution should be avoided; smell is most apparent in slurry stored under anaerobic conditions. Application to land should take account of wind direction ref. housing estates.

There are many husbandry considerations with regard to the application of slurry; the above merely cover the more important legal aspects.

The Pig Welfare Code

While this is only a code of practice it has the approval of Parliament. Anyone found breaking the code and causing distress to pigs, may be prosecuted. The code takes account of the basic needs of pigs viz:

☞ freedom from thirst, hunger and malnutrition
☞ appropriate comfort and shelter
☞ prevention/diagnosis and treatment of disease and injury
☞ freedom from fear
☞ freedom to display normal behaviour

In particular there is great emphasis on the use of straw, on precautions against fire and other emergencies, and on the care needed if slatted floors are used. The code places great emphasis on good stockmanship as a key factor in pig welfare. Legislation has been introduced to phase out the use of stalls/tethers by 1st January 1999.

Welfare Of Livestock Regulations 1990. Alarms & Emergency Ventilation Systems

When livestock are dependent on an automatic ventilation system, there must be an alarm to warn of power or system failure. Alternative means of ventilation must be provided in the event of failure of the automatic (powered) system. All equipment should be checked at least weekly and alarm systems tested every 7 days.

REPRODUCTION

CRITICAL FOR SUCCESS

The correct management of reproduction and fertility is critical for the financial success of any commercial pig unit. The key assessment questions below will be a guide to the overall profitablility of any pig unit.

KEY ASSESSMENT QUESTIONS

	Age at weaning (days)		
	19-25	26-32	33-39
Av. No. Sows & Gilts	**305**	**195**	**162**
Litters/sow/yr	2.26	2.20	2.12
Born alive/litter	10.79	10.86	11.05
Mortality %	11.30	12.80	12.9
Pigs reared/sow/yr	21.6	21.0	20.1
Weaning age (days)	23	27	35
Sow feed/sow/yr (t)	1.3	1.316	1.332

Source: M.L.C. Yearbook 1994

KEY FACTS

Sows Heat Period & Service - Key Facts

☞ **On heat every 20-22 days.**

☞ **It lasts 24 - 60 hrs.**

☞ **Ovulation occurs usually (midway or late) during the heat period and takes 3-4 hours.**

☞ **Produces 18-20 eggs in the mature sows.**

☞ **Sperm stays alive in the sow for about 24 hrs.**

REPRODUCTION

Service Management

Heat detection	twice per day with a boar
Serve	as soon as heat detected*
	every 24 hrs while heat period lasts.*
Supervision	ensures penis enters vulva
	prevent injury to sow (or boar)
Returns	check for these 20 - 22 days after service
Pregnancy test	use doppler machine at 28-35 days after service
(*based on the latest research and will not be typical of most farms)	

Factors Affecting Conception

Gilt management	age = 220 days + on 3rd/4th heat
Condition	needs "fattening" to build up energy reserves
Vaccinations	usually Erysipelas + SMEDI (PARVO)
Sow condition	Condition score 3 or flush
Stress	avoid especially during 12 - 18 days after service.
Boar usage	one sow/week for max. fertility
Post service feeding	2.5 kg/day max. for first month

FARROWING

The sow should be washed and have been treated for parasites; the farrowing pen should be clean, disinfected and dry.

Sows can be induced to farrow (using prostaglandin) in order to supervise farrowing during daytime hours and also to enable batch farrowing to take place and so piglets can be cross-fostered and size graded.

The piglets must be kept in a warm, draught-free creep area (see ⛏). Cold kills, although the end result might appear to be something different, i.e. disease, starvation, overlaying.

REPRODUCTION

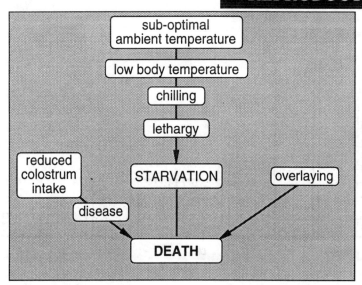

ARTIFICIAL INSEMINATION

As per natural service except use bottle of semen and catheter. There are four organisations from whom semen can be obtained. Most breeding companies now offer semen for sale depending on customer status.

JSR Healthbred Ltd, Selby.

Masterbreeders (A.I. Centre) Ltd, Royston.

Pig Genetics, Thirsk.

Norfolk Pig Breeding Company, Norwich. (UPB Porcofram plc)

Although the use of A.I. in Great Britain has increased substantially over the last 3 years the proportion is still small compared with most European countries viz:

REPRODUCTION

% Of Litters Bred By A. I.

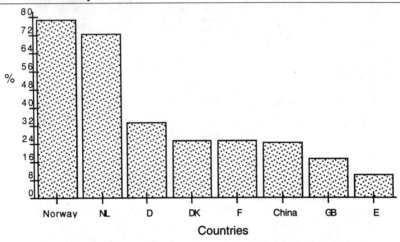

Pig Insemination Using A.I.

When carrying out A.I. in pigs there are 5 spermicides to avoid;

water
urine
blood
detergent
disinfectant

PHYSICAL PERFORMANCE

KEY ASSESSMENT QUESTIONS

Farrowing index	2.4 litters/sow/year
Farrowing rate	90%
Pigs born alive	10.7

Mortality to 3 wks	10%
3 - 7 wks	0.75%
7 - 11 wks	0.75%
after 11 wks	1.5%

Nº pigs born alive	25.68/sow/yr
Nº pigs weaned	23.11
Nº weaners	22.94
Nº growers	22.76
Nº fatteners	22.42

Target weights/ages	5.5 kg @ 3 wks
	15 kg @ 7 wks
	30 kg @ 11 wks
	80 kg @ 19 wks

Liveweight gains	2.5kg/week - weaners
	3.8kg/week - growers
	5.5kg/week - finishers

Food conversion ratios	1.15 from 3 to 7 wks
	1.5 from 7 to 11 wks
	2.7 from 11 to 20 wks

Grading percentages; 1st	90%
2nd	5%
3rd	3%
Misc	2%

GROSS MARGINS

These vary considerably from year to year depending mainly on the pig price (ref supply & demand). In addition the gross margins also vary according to physical performance, food price, and selling weight.

Typical Gross Margin: Pig Breeding And Finishing

Per sow	£
Sales 18.9 @ 88.4 kg slaughter weight @ 83.1p	1388
Less depreciation + mortality	25
OUTPUT	**1363**
Variable costs	
Concentrates Sow	210
Piglet Grower/ finisher	639
Vet & medicine	25
Heat & electricity	27
Water	8
Straw & bedding	6
Sundries	15
Transport	15
TOTAL VARIABLE COSTS	**945**
GROSS MARGIN	**418**

Source: MLC Yearbook '94

Typical Gross Margin: Pig Breeding And Weaning

	Indoor
	£
Sales 22 weaners @ £28.50	627
Less depreciation	26
OUTPUT £	**601**
Variable costs	
Concentrates	
sow (1.24t @ 15p/kg)	186
piglet grower	213
Other variable costs	72
TOTAL VARIABLE COSTS £	**471**
GROSS MARGIN £	**130**

Source:A.B.C. 1994.

NOTE:

whilst gross margins are broadly similar for indoor and outdoor systems, fixed costs in outdoor systems are about 50% of those for indoor systems and this should be taken into consideration:

Capital/sow (£)	Outdoor	233
Buildings and Equipment (£)	Indoor	435

PERFORMANCE

Gross Margin Per Sow Adjusted For Inflation

NOTE: The Gross Margin Results reflects cyclical changes in price levels.

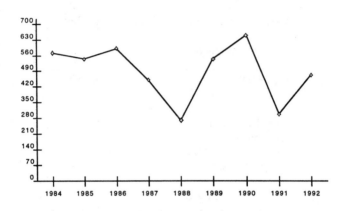

Source: Adapted from M.L.C. Yearbook 1993

FIXED COSTS

The level of fixed costs vary considerably, largely due to the level of fixed capital investment and subsequent depreciation/financial charges. Average figures for fixed costs for the selling weights below might be as follows:

Selling weight kg	Fixed costs/sow £
65 - 75	133
75 - 85	122
85 - 100	125

Labour is probably the major element of fixed costs (£150 - £180/sow bacon production) but financial and capital charges (depreciation, interest and loan repayments) can be higher and crippling.

Weaner production could produce gross margins of approximately **50%** of those achieved by selling pigs at 85 - 100 kgs l.wt. and have approx **half the level of fixed costs.**

THE
OUTSIDER'S GUIDE
to
OUTDOOR PIGS

1995 Edition

PRODUCTION

The domesticated pig has been derived mainly, and in varying proportions, from the European species *SUS SCROFA*, and *SUS VITATUS* the pot-bellied, small, black pig of sub-tropical and tropical S.E. Asia.

The pig is a very versatile animal and is kept under varying climatic conditions throughout the world. It is found in small herds kept outdoors, owned by peasant farmers and in large intensive indoor units in Western Europe. The diet may consist of grass, forages and roots or cereals and highly digestible proteins. Generally in the Western world pigs are kept intensively, while in the rest of the world they are kept as foragers or scavengers eating cheap, by-product type foods. There is now however, a trend in the UK back towards outdoor pig production.

THE WORLD

million tonnes

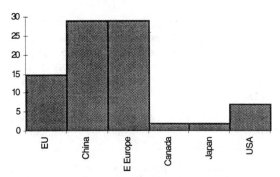

World Production (selected countries)

The pig is the main source of meat for human consumption.

World ProductionOf Meat

	'000 M/tonnes	%
Pigs	72571	41
Cattle types	53293	29
Poultry	43046	24
Sheep/goats	9902	6
Total	**178812**	**100**

Source: F.A.O.

OUTSIDER'S GUIDE

Production And Consumption

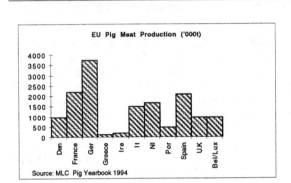

EU Pig Meat Production ('000t)

Source: MLC Pig Yearbook 1994

In the EU during the last few years consumption of pigmeat per head of the population has increased from 40kg to 41kg/head/year. Self sufficiency in the EU over the same period has been 100% to 103% resulting in a very small surplus for storage

THE UNITED KINGDOM

Why Outdoor Pigs?

Historically the domesticated pig in Britain was used as a scavenger. There is a reference in the Domesday Book to a privilege called 'pannage' - pigs being allowed to forage in manorial woods living off acorns, roots and a wide variety of vegetation. Later on pigs were kept in cottage sties and after this there was a gradual movement to the intensive housing systems seen today.

Current indoor systems are extremely capital intensive. A new indoor unit on a greenfield site would show a return on capital significantly less than could be obtained from a safe bank or building society deposit account.

The main reasons for the revival in interest in outdoor weaner production are:

> **attractive return on capital**
>
> **low maintenance costs**
>
> **alternative land using enterprise**
>
> **improved public image regarding welfare**
>
> **potential free range price premium**
>
> **boost to soil fertility**

Main Outdoor Pig Requirements:

A free-draining soil and low rainfall. Given these and new technology learnt from indoor pig units, new equipment (fencing, hut design, all-terrain vehicles) and the new hybrid gilts now available, the outdoor system can be a most attractive form of production, assuming reasonable production figures.

PRODUCTION

Consumption

Consumption has has shown a slight increase to 21kg per head, with pork consumption increasing at the expense of bacon and ham.

Production

DISTRIBUTION OF ALL PIGS IN THE UK

These figures are average county densities and NOT stocking rates

Outdoor pigs may be found all over the UK on suitable soils and in low rainfall areas but...

0 - 14 / 100 ha

15 - 39 / 100 ha

75 - 149/100 ha

40 - 74/100 ha

over 70% of outdoor Pigs are in 4 counties

Currently the UK is 102% self-sufficient in pork and so is a small exporter. However; being only 42% self-sufficient in bacon and ham, 29% of bacon supplies come from Denmark and 22% from the Netherlands.

The Pig Cycle

Pigs reach puberty at 6 months and have a short pregnancy of four months and are very prolific (10 reared per litter).

This means that the size of the breeding herd and therefore the number of slaughter pigs can vary considerably from one year to the next.

There is virtually no price support mechanism in the UK and thus, with a static demand for pigmeat (unlike in the EU 12) any over supply will have a big effect on price. Any high price triggers expansion and the market becomes rapidly over supplied and prices drop.

Monthly Average All Pig Price (A.A.P.P.) /kg deadweight

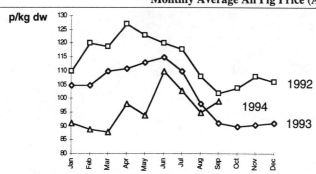

p/kg dw

1992
1994
1993

Source: M.L.C Oct '94

PRODUCTION

KEY ASSESSMENT QUESTIONS

	Outdoor breeding	Indoor breeding
Farrowing index (litters/sow/year)	2.20	2.26
Pigs born alive/litter	10.82	10.80
Mortality of pigs born alive(%)	11.4	11.9
Pigs reared/sow/yr	21.1	21.5
Weaning age (days)	24.00	25.00
Sow feed per sow per year (t)	1.43	1.24

FACTORS AFFECTING SOW PROFITABILITY

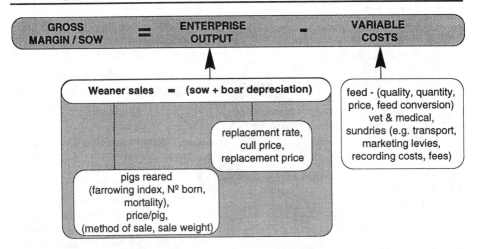

```
GROSS          =    ENTERPRISE    -    VARIABLE
MARGIN / SOW        OUTPUT             COSTS
```

Weaner sales — (sow + boar depreciation)

replacement rate,
cull price,
replacement price

pigs reared
(farrowing index, Nº born,
mortality),
price/pig,
(method of sale, sale weight)

feed - (quality, quantity,
price, feed conversion)
vet & medical,
sundries (e.g. transport,
marketing levies,
recording costs, fees)

Note: Similar factors affect the profitability of fattener pig (bacon, pork) production.

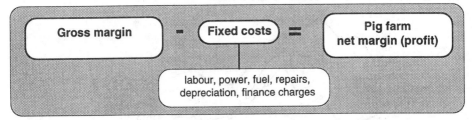

Gross margin — Fixed costs = Pig farm
net margin (profit)

labour, power, fuel, repairs,
depreciation, finance charges

THE PRODUCTION CYCLE

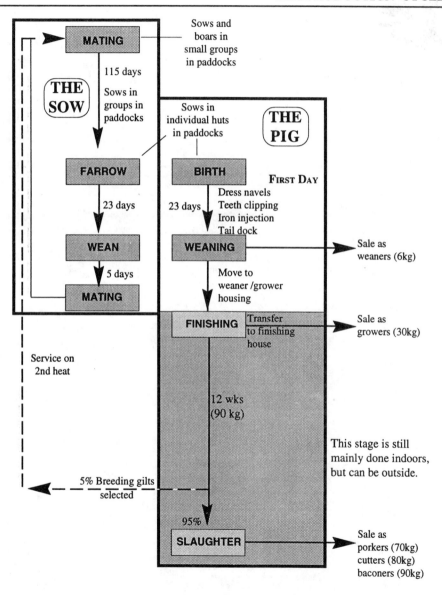

MATING — Sows and boars in small groups in paddocks

THE SOW

115 days

Sows in groups in paddocks

Sows in individual huts in paddocks

THE PIG

FARROW

BIRTH — First Day
Dress navels
Teeth clipping
Iron injection
Tail dock

23 days

23 days

WEAN

WEANING → Sale as weaners (6kg)

5 days

Move to weaner/grower housing

MATING

FINISHING — Transfer to finishing house → Sale as growers (30kg)

Service on 2nd heat

12 wks (90 kg)

This stage is still mainly done indoors, but can be outside.

5% Breeding gilts selected

95%

SLAUGHTER → Sale as porkers (70kg) cutters (80kg) baconers (90kg)

PRODUCTION

MARKETING

PRODUCTS

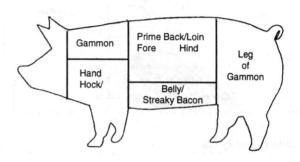

Outdoor System Products

The majority of outdoor producers are using a Duroc X Landrace sow. It is important to select the right breed of sow that is not only hardy but will produce lean carcasses.

Weaners: most outdoor units sell weaners either:

i   **at weaning (6kg)** straight out of the field or

ii **at 25 - 30kg** having been grown-on
    a   in buildings on the farmstead
    b   huts in the field.

Pig diagram labels: Gammon, Prime Back/Loin (Fore, Hind), Leg of Gammon, Hand Hock/, Belly/ Streaky Bacon

MARKET OUTLETS

Outdoor weaned pigs can be sold either through a marketing group or co-operative to arable farms for growing and fattening. These pigs are normally stronger, fitter and healthier than pigs bred indoors.

MARKET INFORMATION

Carcass Information

The M.L.C., acting as an independent organization, classify (i.e. grade) about 80% of all clean pig carcasses and young boar carcasses.

Carcasses are **dressed** to the agreed specification (liveweight minus specific offals) and the following measurement/assessments are made upon which abattoirs base their grade and price:

OUTSIDER'S GUIDE

MARKETING

M.L.C. Grading

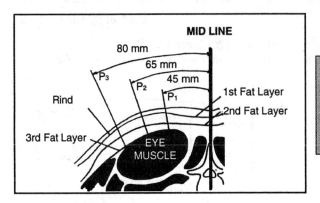

cold carcass weight
backfat thickness (usually P_2 or P_1 & P_3)
visible carcass faults
length (optional)
conformation (optional)

Abattoirs And Prices

There are about 700 abattoirs in Great Britain which are involved in slaughtering pigs; of these 60 are specialist pig abattoirs.

There is no direct price support mechanism/subsidy for UK producers. Abattoirs determine their own prices for the respective grades/carcass weight and these are usually related to the weekly average all pigs price (A.A.P.P.). The **A.A.P.P.** is published each week in the farming press and fluctuates according to supply and demand.

A guide to fat depths, grades and prices can be seen below:

Weights, Prices & Gradings (P_2)

Lwt kg	KO% %	D wt kg	Grades (mm - P_2- fat)				
			first	second	third	fourth	fifth
55-68	72	40.5-50	7-11	13	15	17	17+
Price	=	A.A.P.P.	+11p	+9p	+7p	+3p	-1p
68-80	74	50.5-60	7-12	14	16	18	18+
Price	=	A.A.P.P.	+7p	+5p	+3p	-1p	-5p
80-85	75	60.5-63	7-12	14	16	18	
Price	=	A.A.P.P.	+4p	+2p	-1p	-7p	
85-98	76	63.5-75	7-14	15	17	19+	
Price	=	A.A.P.P.	0	-2p	-5p	-13p	

Levies

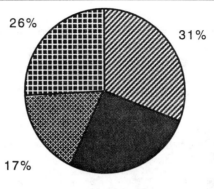

All slaughter pigs carry a levy of approximately 90p/ pig which is collected by M.L.C. for promotion and a general levy (R+D). Carcass classification is calculated on a local basis.

26%

31%   Carcass classification 31%

Pig meat promotion 26%

Research & development 17%

Meat inspection 26%

17%

26%

EU Regulations

A pig carcass grading scheme was introduced in January 1989 to cover all pigs slaughtered within the EU.

The basis of this scheme is lean meat content. At present, until most abattoirs acquire new measuring equipment this will be calculated from the fat measurement of the carcass in relation to its weight and there will be no compulsion on the abattoirs to pay for carcasses on a % lean meat basis.

The New Grading Regime (Definitions Of Conformation & Fatness)

Grade		% Lean meat
S		>60
E	Excellent	55-60
U	Very good	50-55
R	Good	45-50
O	Fair	40-45
P	Poor	< 40

MARKETING

Male Pigs

The majority of male pigs sold entire (not castrated) with advantages of:

> **faster growth rate**
> **food conversion ratio**
> **improved gradings**

INTRODUCTION

Breeding stock need to be capable of producing **large numbers of pigs** with **quick** and **efficient growth** into **lean carcasses**. Hardiness and mothering ability are two further requirements specific to the outdoor pigs herd.

Breed Improvement

Currently the leading breeding companies are maintaining two lines ('male' and 'female') within each breed population in order to maximize the rate of genetic improvement. One line is used to produce males where selection is made on growth efficiency and leanness, whilst the other line is used to produce females where selection is based on prolificacy and mothering ability.

DAM LINES

SIRE LINES

NEW
F₁ PARENT GILT

NEW BOAR

Boars and gilts with high levels of performance in these traits are given high indices; however, each breeding company operates a different index range, thus pigs from one company cannot be compared with pigs from another.

Main Breeds

CHARACTERISTICS			ECONOMIC STRENGTHS/WEAKNESSES					
Breed	**Coat**	**Ears**	**P**	**M**	**H**	**GR**	**FCR**	**L**
L. White	White	pricked	+	av	+	+	+	av
Landrace	White	lop	+	av	av	+	+	av
Welsh	White	lop	+	av	av	+	+	av
Duroc	Ginger	lop	av	+	+	av	av	+
Hampshire	Black. White & Saddle	pricked	-	av	+	-	-	+
British Saddleback	Black. White & Saddle	lop	-	+	+	-	-	-
Pietrain	White & black spots	lop	-	-	-	-	-	+
Key:	P=prolific; M=mothering ability; H=hardiness; GR=growth rate; FCR=food conversion ratio; L=lean; '+' indicates better than average.							

BREEDS & SYSTEMS

COMMERCIAL OBJECTIVES

Most breeding companies are now producing a 'purpose-bred' outdoor gilt which is capable of producing:

> **large litters**
>
> **pigs with efficient growth**
>
> **pigs with relatively lean carcasses**

The typical, **modern** outdoor gilt consists of Landrace and Duroc breeds with or without dashes of one or two other breeds.

Higher the proportion of Duroc in the hybrid female will mean that the progeny are hardier but the gilt/sows are more difficult to handle.

Cross-bred terminal sires have a better reproductive performance and produce more lean meat in the carcasses of their progeny than pure-bred terminal sires and are therefore probably a slightly better bet with outdoor herds.

On-Farm Policy

 Flying Herd Policy

The herd consists entirely of F1 hybrid females purchased from breeding companies or private breeders. New stock should be isolated and then integrated into the herd to prevent health risks to the existing herd and/or the new stock. Most outdoor herds come into this category.

D.I.Y. Policy

Very few outdoor herds breed their own replacement gilts / boars. The pure bred (grand parent) lines are less hardy than their hybrid progeny and therefore only if they can be housed indoors should the D.I.Y. policy be contemplated.

KEY ASSESSMENT QUESTIONS

Breeding	Av.	Top 10%		
Average weaning age (days)	24	23		
Sow feed/sow/year (t)	1.43	1.42		
Feed/pig reared; Sow feed (kg)	74	70		
Creep feed (kg)	0.1	0.2		
Rearing (6 to 25 kg)				
Feed conversion ratio	1.70	1.50		
Daily gain (g)	400	425		
Feed/pig reared (kg) 32	28			
Feeding (25 kg to disposal)				
Slaughterweight (kg)	72	85	92	100
Finishing period (weeks)	10	12.5	13.5	15
Feed conversion rate (Av.)	2.4	2.7	2.75	3
Food/pig (kg)	113	162	184	225
Daily liveweight gain (g/day)	670	712	712	714

Source: M.L.C.

NUTRITION

FEEDING PIGS

Pigs are single-stomach animals able to utilise a wide range of foods. In the UK, **hybrid pigs** are usually **fed high energy cereal** diets balanced with supplementary protein, minerals and vitamins. **Main feed constituents** are wheat, barley, soya bean and other vegetable proteins. They may also be fed potatoes, swedes, turnips etc.

FEEDING AIMS

Breeding Stock

Maintain the breeding stock in a healthy and fit condition to achieve up to **2.5 production cycles** per annum on **three to four week weaning**.

Gilts

At **six months** on average, gilts reach puberty or first heat. The best practice should be for **first mating to occur** at the **3rd heat** or **4th heat** having being fed ad lib from purchase up to this time so that they have a long and productive breeding life and so that they acquire a good layer of insulation. Ad lib feeders should be situated in the maiden gilt paddocks. Gilts should be minimum of 210/220 days old and weigh 130/140 kg at service.

The Sows

Service

Gilts and sows should be fed ad lib from ad lib feeders in the service paddock. Boar condition should be watched carefully.

Dry period

Dry sows are normally fed about 3kg food per day in roll or cob form and this is usually spread on the ground.

Lactation

Relatively high levels of energy feed intake (6 - 8 kg/day sow nuts) are required to maintain condition for the next breeding cycle. Again, sows should be fed ad lib from ad lib feeders.

NUTRITION

Sow Feeding Scales

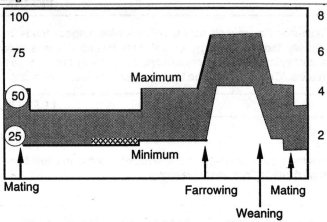

Maximum and minimum levels of energy intake by sow. The area between the two levels represents the range of choices available and depends on sow condition. In the case of outdoor sows, the energy intake is likely to be near the maximum.

Boars

General aim is to keep them in a hard, fit lean condition. Overweight boars are lazy, slow to work and too heavy for smaller sows and gilts. Generally they need working in short bursts in the service paddock for a few days and then swapped for another group of boars to ensure maximum fertility.

Suckling Pigs

The **AIM** is to maximize new born pigs' disease resistance. It is essential that they ingest as much **colostrum** as possible to obtain protective antibodies **within the first 6 hours**.

Have clean **water available** at all times to increase dry matter intake. Sweetening agents can be added to encourage intake. Creep feed if fed should be changed at least once/day to maintain freshness and encourage eating.

RECOMMENDED FEED LEVELS

Typical Diet Specifications

Units	D.E./kg MJ	Oil %	Fibre %	Protein %	Lysine %	Cost/t £
Outdoor sow						
Cobs/rolls	13.2	5	5	17	0.8	165
Pellets	13.5	5	5	17	0.8	165

Typical Feed Amounts

Units	Body Wt. kg	Energy MJ DE/day	Feed intake kg	Diet type
Dry sows	140	35	3.0	Sow
Lact. sows	140	90	ad lib	Sow
Gilts	90	35	ad lib	Sow
Boar	160	35	3.0	Sow

NUTRITION

HEALTH

INTRODUCTION

There are probably more diseases that affect pigs than any other species of farm livestock. Furthermore, still many diseases are viral in origin and cannot be cured by antibiotic therapy.

In outdoor herds disease problems are likely to be less severe (e.g. respiratory problems) but effective disease control methods must still be set up and followed.

SOURCES OF DISEASE

There is no single disease which is of more concern to the pig manager than any other. The most important thing is **prevention**.

This means strict hygiene methods which apply to **EVERYONE GOING ONTO A PIG UNIT**, especially company representatives or anyone going from farm to farm.

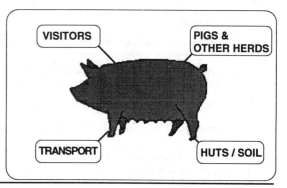

DISEASE PREVENTION

Herd Health Security

i   Visitors do not enter unit without permission and:

should be kept to a minimum;
may need 24 hrs. clearance from pigs;
wear units own boots/overalls;
use foot dips.

ii Transport food lorries should blow food into bins without entry onto the unit:

pig wagons should load up at perimeter;
knacker wagon should collect off-site;
misc. vehicles, if necessary, have wheel dip/spray.

iii Replacement breeding stock require isolation.

iv Huts and soil.

Farrowing huts (also known as arcs or bungalows) must be moved to clean soil between litters and the herd should be moved at least once every two years.

It is essential in hot weather to provide wallows and/or shade. Apart from causing excessive stress and perhaps death, excessive heat (25° C+) will lead to infertility problems.

Vaccination Programme

All vaccines should be stored at 3-8° C and generally, if a bottle is opened, it should be emptied.

i Erysipelas

Erysipelas is caused by bacteria which can survive for years in organic matter. It does not always cause the classic purple, diamond marks on the skin. It is also responsible for abortions, arthritis and death through heart attacks. All breeding stock (including boars) should be vaccinated at least twice a year.

ii S.M.E.D.I.

Caused by parvo-viruses which inhabit the uterus of gilts/sows and affect reproductive performance without causing the pig herself any illness. It results in stillbirths, mummified piglets, embryonic mortality (small litters) or infertility. All breeding stock, including boars, should undergo a routine vaccination programme.

iii Other diseases

These may be prevented by a vaccination policy depending on specific problems/ veterinary advice.

Miscellaneous Preventative Measures

i Parasites

All breeding stock should be routinely treated for worms, lice and mange, usually twice a year with one of the many proprietary products available.

ii Anaemia

All baby piglets should be given iron to prevent anaemia as the sows milk is naturally deficient in iron. Although some iron is obtained from the soil, it is somewhat unreliable as a method to prevent anaemia.

iii Routine vet visits

Very useful as an aid to preventing disease.

iv Lameness and injury

Problems can occur if ground conditions are unsuitable, especially in the serving paddock. Biotin in the sows' ration may help to prevent hoof damage, but other wise local injuries and cuts should be treated with sprays or injection of antibiotics.

v Heat stroke

Pigs are particularly sensitive to heat - they have no covering of fur or wool, and they cannot sweat to keep cool. Shade and wallows should be provided in hot weather.

SOME NOTIFIABLE DISEASES

Anthrax

Very rare but is of bacterial origin and usually results in death.

Aujesky's Disease

A virus causing abortion in pregnant sows and scours together with high mortality rates in young pigs.

Foot and Mouth Disease

A virus causing blisters on the feet and tongue of cloven-footed animals.

Swine Fever

Highly contagious virus disease usually resulting in a high fever and death.

Swine Vesicular Disease

Virus causing very similar symptoms to Foot and Mouth Disease.

SOME COMMON DISEASES

Piglet Scours

Can be nutritional (usually yellow) but often is of bacterial or viral origin. The most common cause is a bacteria called E. coli, of which there are many strains.

Meningitis

Caused by a bacteria which can often be treated with penicillin if caught early enough. Usually associated with stress of weaning but other stresses include moving, mixing, temperature, low ventilation rates. Symptoms include unco-ordinated movement and then death.

Enzootic Pneumonia

Is an infection of the lungs caused by a virus. Leads to coughing, loss of condition and eventually perhaps death.

Atrophic Rhinitis

Deformation/destruction of the turbinate bones in the nostrils. Symptoms include twisted snouts, runny eyes and sneezing, and often leads to other secondary infections of the respiratory tract.

Swine Dysentery

A disease of growing/finishing pigs caused by a type of virus. It is easily spread in houses that have dung scraped along the length of the dung passageway. Symptoms are blood stained scouring.

Mastitis/Metritis/Agalactia (M.M.A.)

This is a post-farrowing disorder of sows. It is multi-factoral in origin, and often leads to a shortage of milk (hence piglet mortality) and sometimes subsequent infertility in the sows after weaning.

HEALTH

LEGAL ASPECTS

Code For The Use Of Medicines

i Source

Obtain products only from veterinary surgeons or registered agricultural merchants.

ii Storage

Temperature and light can be critical. Some products must be kept under lock/key.

iii Records

Must be kept of purchases and use (date, quantity, stock). In some cases empty bottles must be returned to supplier.

iv Withdrawal times

Withdrawal periods are laid down for specific products relating to the time between the end of the treatment and the date of slaughter. It is important to avoid certain residues in meat for human consumption.

Miscellaneous

Casualty pigs must be certified free from antibodies, fit to travel, the carcass must be free from infection and suitable for human consumption as outlined in the new meat inspection regulations introduced in January 1991.

OUTDOOR SYSTEMS

There is a wide range and combination of housing system, and paddock layout. Outdoor systems vary from farm to farm because of:

> herd size
>
> soil type
>
> shape and extent of land available
>
> the possible use of farm buildings for part of the production cycle (e.g. indoor serving, housing weaners indoors)

The system can however, be completely carried out outdoors and can move around an arable farm giving a significant boost to soil fertility. The only requirement is that there should always be water available for the herd where ever it is located.

For a complete outdoor system, the stocking rate can range between 12 - 25 sows per hectare, the higher figure being possible on very light land where the piglets are moved off the paddock at weaning.

PADDOCK LAYOUT

Over recent years two main paddock layouts have emerged, namely conventional or radial layouts. Both systems require four categories of paddock:

> gilts
>
> service
>
> dry sows
>
> farrowing

Conventional Paddock Layout

Paddocks are laid out to fit into existing field boundaries. All shapes and sizes of fields can be used. Roads and trackways should be fitted in to reduce travelling time and to permit good access for feeding and pig movements.

Radial Paddock Layout

This is a very recent development for outdoor pig production. Paddocks are laid out radially with a small centre circle made of hurdles for handling and moving stock. One big advantage of this system is that **stock can be moved easily** by one man and without expensive hydraulically operated trailers and large tractors.

HOUSING

The system does require a **large area of open field** without hedges or ditches etc. running across the site. The perimeter fence need not be circular but can fit the shape of the field to some extent.

The **central circle holds** a small 'caravan' which can be used as an office, store and also a container to hold small stocks of food in the event of bad weather.

This layout makes for an **efficient use of labou**r - one man can look after 250 sows which is probably as many as one would require in one unit.

SOW RADIAL PADDOCK

---

250 SOW RADIAL PADDOCK

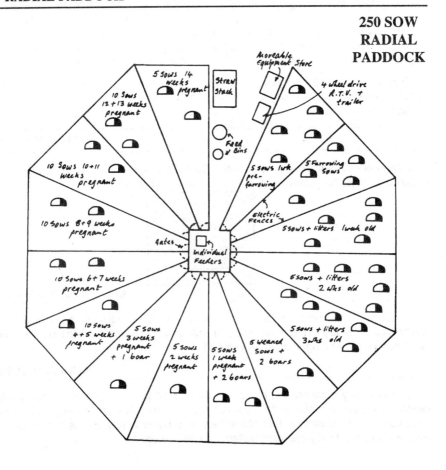

EQUIPMENT

Housing

The traditional design has largely remained unchanged over the years. This is galvanised zinc sheeting with wooden ends on a wooden or metal frame. The huts need to be strong so that they will stand moving, heavy so that they will not blow away and yet light enough so that they may be lifted and moved by one man (farrowing hut). They should not have a floor.

Farrowing Huts

Some manufacturers fit farrowing rails to their farrowing huts to reduce crushing injuries, while most have some sort of **fender** arrangement to prevent the baby piglets getting lost, and to prevent cross suckling.

Recently, an insulated farrowing hut has been developed. This encourages sows to suckle in warm weather. Huts may also be obtained in a **plastic-like** material, but while they are very light, they need pegging down and are also more expensive when setting up a unit.

Water Trough

Each paddock should have a water trough which may double up as a wallow bath, or produce a wallow area in hot spells of weather. A seperate wallow should be provided to allow pigs to keep cool in hot weather. Shade is also beneficial.

Miscellaneous

Capital investment

A tractor, all-terrain vehicle (A.T.V.) and trailer or landrover is required to move food, straw and weaners. A small caravan or container may also be useful. **However, it is essential to keep capital investment to a minimum.**

Weaners

If weaners are grown on in the paddock, then more land and huts are required. If weaners go indoors, then muck handling equipment and a power washer are required.

Fencing

One of the main factors in the increase in interest in outdoor production is the development of light weight electric fencing systems. It is now cheaper, versatile and reliable and very effective. The fence unit may be powered by battery or mains electricity. Batteries may be replaceable, or recharged by wind.

Two strands are required at 200 mm and 500 mm above ground level. A small training paddock suitably enclosed by pig netting is advisable for newly acquired stock.

Feeding And Watering

Ad-lib feeders, suitably bird-proofed, are required for the maiden gilt paddock, the service and the farrowing paddocks. Sow cobs can be fed to the sows on the ground.

CAPITAL PROFILE - 250 SOW UNIT SELLING 30KG WEANERS

Item	Nº of units	Unit price £	Subtotal £	Total £
Farrowing huts	60	210	12600	
Dry sow huts, Boar				
Gilt huts	38	180	6840	19440
Water pipes (m)				
Throughs, fittings	-	-	2660	2660
Electric fence (A.C.)				
Pig netting				
Hurdles	-	-	3300	3300
ATV/2nd hand tractor	1	3000	3000	
Livestock trailer	1	1250	1250	
Water bowser	1	200	200	
Feed trailer	1	1560	1560	
Small tools	1	600	600	
Fuel tank	1	120	120	
Feed bins	1	1200	1200	7930
Rearing Units	18	1040	18720	18720
Grand total				£ 52050
Total per sow				£ 208.20

LEGAL REQUIREMENTS

**Water Act 1989, Environmental Protection Act 1990,
Control Of Pollution Regulations 1991**

Legislation which may affect the application of manures and other wastes (including afterbirths and dead pigs) is wide ranging and covered by several Acts of Parliament. The main provisions are:

i   direct discharge (or indirect seepage) of farm wastes to water courses is forbidden. Organic matter can cause de-oxygenation of water, resulting in death of fish/plants; disease organisms can be spread via water courses

ii   pollution of ground waters should be avoided if water is extracted for human consumption

iii atmospheric pollution should be avoided; smell is most apparent in slurry stored under anaerobic conditions. Application to land should take account of wind direction ref. housing estates.

There are many husbandry considerations with regard to the application of slurry; the above merely cover the more important legal aspects.

The Pig Welfare Code

While this is only a code of practice it has the approval of Parliament. Anyone found breaking the code and causing distress to pigs, may be prosecuted. The code takes account of the basic needs of pigs viz:

☞ freedom from thirst, hunger and malnutrition

☞ appropriate comfort and shelter

☞ prevention/diagnosis and treatment of disease and injury

☞ freedom from fear

☞ freedom to display normal behaviour

Miscellaneous

A current E. U. directive recommends that nitrogen application should be limited to 170kg per ha per year. This, if implemented, would restrict the stocking rates to about 10/ha.

OUTSIDER'S GUIDE

HOUSING

CRITICAL FOR SUCCESS

The correct management of reproduction and fertility is critical for the financial success of any commercial pig unit. The key facts below should form the basis of the serving system.

SOWS HEAT PERIOD AND SERVICE - KEY FACTS

- On heat every 20-22 days
- It lasts 24 - 60 hrs
- Ovulation occurs sometime (early, midway or late) during the heat period and takes 3-4 hours
- Sroduces 18-20 eggs in the mature sows
- Sperm stays alive in the sow for about 24 hrs
- Optimum rest period for boar 4 days

SERVICE MANAGEMENT

While controlled heat detection and serving is practised on indoor units, this is not the case outdoors. In order to achieve maximum fertility, more boars are required i.e. 1 boar to 10 - 12 sows.

Normally boars are kept in groups or squads of 3 to 4 boars and are rotated around the service paddocks. A group of boars is introduced to a group of freshly weaned sows and stays in that paddock for 3 - 4 days. They are then moved into another paddock when all or the majority of sows have been served. Some units are using individual weaned sow paddocks to allow individual service (1:1 Boar:Sow Ratio) to boost litter size.

'Rested' boars are then moved into the weaned sows for another period of 3 - 4 days and in this way an adequate number of fresh boars are always running with sows due for service.

After service, the sows normally stay in the same dry sow paddock throughout gestation, and the other boars are moved around as needed. A squad of 3 - 4 young boars run with a group of gilts when required. As squads of boars are broken up because of culling, through injury etc. the single ones are used as chaser boars in the dry sow paddocks. Some units are pregnancy testing to improve output.

Large herds may wean twice a week in order to spread the serving load; sows can then be grouped for feeding purposes. At weaning, most vaccinations are carried out (not Smedi) and any missing rings, or ear tags are replaced.

REPRODUCTION

FACTORS AFFECTING CONCEPTION

Gilt management	Ad lib feed to increase condition - performance and hardiness
Vaccinations	Erysipelas and SMEDI (twice per year).
Sow condition	Ad lib feed at weaning to service. Ad lib feeding in farrowing paddocks.
Boar management	Rotate squads to maintain fresh supply of semen.
Post service	Maximum feed intake 2.5 kg/day.

FARROWING

For herds weaning at 21 - 24 days of age there should be five farrowing paddocks - 3 with suckling pigs, one with in-pig sows and one being cleaned - huts moved, and stood on end for the rain to wash and the straw burnt.

Farrowing Hut And Fender

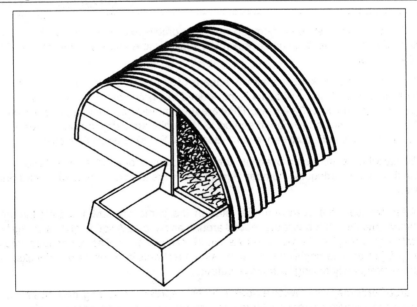

REPRODUCTION

The aim is to farrow all the sows in the paddock within a short 3 - 4 day periods in order to facilitate weaning; any sows not conforming are moved to the next farrowing paddock. Usually service dates are not observed and it is assumed sows are served around five days after weaning.

A sow is usually brought into the farrowing paddock 'by eye' several days early and allowed to find her own hut, and maintain her territory around the hut. Hence rows of huts are placed twenty metres apart with their entrances facing north east which reduces the amount of wind and rain entering the huts.

Supervision of farrowing is seldom practised; disturbing the sow especially in the dark, does more harm than good. After all the sows have farrowed the ad lib feeders are filled and the sows can eat to appetite. Fenders keep the piglets in the farrowing hut and prevent straying.

Piglet Tasks

These include teeth clipping, tail docking, iron injection and fostering if necessary.

The piglets need to be kept warm, but too much straw leads to overlaying / crushing; plastic curtain strips over the entrance are a good idea.

REPRODUCTION

PHYSICAL PERFORMANCE

Recording

Recorded information is essential for the production of performance data on which herd management decisions are made.

The outdoor herd needs a record collection system that is basically waterproof - perhaps a small pocket notepad / pencil (or taperecorder). This information is then transferred to the main input cards and is then ready for processing with manual or computer methods.

One specific problem with outdoor herds is that most services are not supervised and the majority may well be observed only from a distance. Therefore, it is normal to assume that all sows are served in the first week after weaning and to record accordingly. Likewise with squads of boars it is difficult to pick up any individual fertility problem.

Identification

Ear tagging is the most popular system of identification, usually one in each ear. Different colours can be used to highlight different production criteria.

Notching as tags aids identification in bad weather.

RECORDING SYSTEMS AND COSTS

On-Farm Computer Recording Schemes

Company	Program 1	Cost £	Program 2	Cost £
Amplan	Sowplan	350	Hamplan	300
HM Boot	Pigpro	800	Pig Management System	2000
Easicare	Easycare 1	800	Easycare 2	450
	Healthcare	500	Accounts	350
Hylton Nomis	Pig Program	2000	-	-
LKL Services	Logiporc Breeding	900	Logiporc Feeding	850
Armada	Pig Man	850	-	-
Pig Breeders Supply Co.	Pig Champ	850	-	-
Sum it	Pig Manage't	350	-	-

PERFORMANCE

Annual Costs Per Sow Of Bureau Systems (£)

System		Herd size			
	150	200	250	300	500
Pigtales (subsidised herds £1.00 per sow less)	4.50	4.50	4.50	4.40	4.00
Easicare 1+ 2 (15% discount for advanced payment)	4.21	3.82	3.52	3.47	3.18
M.L.C. Pigplan	2.10	1.80	1.62	1.50	1.08
M.L.C. Sow & Boar	2.80	2.80	2.80	2.80	2.80
Sowgen	3.60	3.60	3.60	3.60	3.60

(1990)

OUTSIDER'S GUIDE

PHYSICAL PERFORMANCE

KEY ASSESSMENT QUESTIONS

Item	1993	1994
Herd structure		
Av. Nº sows & Gilts	217	449
Sow performance		
Litters/sow/year	2.26	2.27
Pigs born alive/sow/yr	10.73	10.82
Mortality (%)	12.1	11.4
Pigs reared/sow/yr	21.3	21.1
Av. days @ weaning	25	23
Feed usage		
Sow feed/sow/yr (t)	1.230	1.42

Source: M.L.C. Year Book 1993

GROSS MARGIN

Typical Gross Margin - 32 kg Weaner Production

Per Sow		£
Sales Weaners - 21 @ £28/weaner		588
Less depreciation		22
OUTPUT		**566**
Variable costs		
Feed	sow	205
	piglet/grower	196
Other Variable costs		67
TOTAL VARIABLE COSTS		**468**
GROSS MARGIN		**98**

Source: ABC 1994

PERFORMANCE

NOTE:

Whilst gross margins are broadly similar for indoor and outdoor systems, fixed costs in outdoor systems are about 50% of those for indoor systems and this should be taken into consideration.

	Outdoor £	Indoor £
Capital/sow (£) for Buildings and Equipment	233	435
Cost comparisons (sow/year)		
Labour (hours)	108	148
Land charges	10	3
Buildings & Equipment	24	35
Other fixed costs	33	66

Source: J. Nix, 1994

THE
OUTSIDER'S GUIDE
to
SHEEP

1995 Edition

PRODUCTION

THE INDUSTRY

The UK is the largest producer of sheep in the European community. The UK is also amongst the top five exporters of sheep meat in the world, exporting 140,000 tonnes of the 358,000 tonnes produced.

Many British sheep are kept on the hill and upland regions in the west and north of the UK. This is where, because of poor growing conditions, other kinds of farming and animal rearing are unsuitable. Ewes are also kept in the arable lowland pastures, and generally integrated with other enterprises such as dairying.

THE WORLD

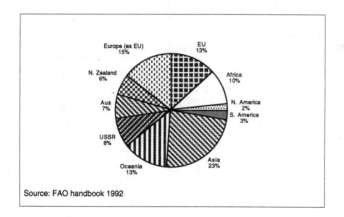

Source: FAO handbook 1992

Total world production 7,029 million tonnes.

EUROPE

Consumption And Self Sufficiency

Consumption - this has risen steadily in recent years.

Self sufficiency - currently the EU is about 80% self sufficient. The bulk of the shortfall is imported from New Zealand.

OUTSIDER'S GUIDE

European Production Of Sheepmeat 1993 ('000t)

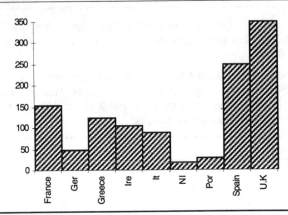

THE UNITED KINGDOM

Sheep have been relatively profitable since the UK joined the EU, and as a result sheep numbers have risen by 45% from 1971 to 1988 to reach **20 m ewes**. There has been a slight increase in the last two years.

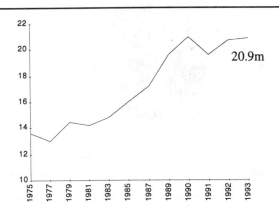

20.9m

The UK Flock

Breeding Ewes	46.7%
Rams	1.1%
Lambs < 1 year	50.1%
Others	2.1%
TOTAL	**43.9 million**

PRODUCTION

Average flock size
= 400 ewes

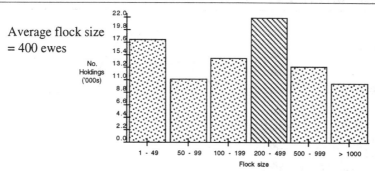

No. Holdings ('000s)

Flock size: 1 - 49, 50 - 99, 100 - 199, 200 - 499, 500 - 999, > 1000

Distribution Of Stock Within The UK

Hill areas (45%)

Poor land, harsh climate, low stocking rates, extensive systems of management. Sheep often the only form of enterprise. Average flock size = 1000 ewes.

Upland areas (38%)

Conditions more favourable than hills, but less than lowland. Average flock size 700 ewes.

Lowland areas (17%)

Fertile land, kinder climate, high stocking rates, intensive management systems. Sheep one of several enterprises, usually in a mixed farm situation. Often utilising arable by-products. Average flock size 500 ewes.

Nº sheep per 100 ha agricultural land

108

98   252

113

47   122

394   69

113   75

PRODUCTION

PRODUCTION OF SHEEPMEAT ('000 TONNES)

Currently the UK produces:

80% of its lamb requirement;

Shortfalls are made up by imports, chiefly from New Zealand.

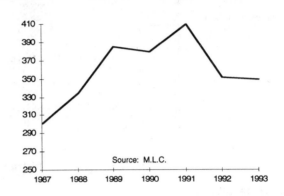

Source: M.L.C.

Consumption

Consumption of sheepmeat has declined dramatically in the UK largely due to:

- concern over dangers of red meat in the diet;
- concern over use of antibiotics/hormones;
- lamb is regarded as fatty and wasteful;
- rise in popularity of convenience foods.

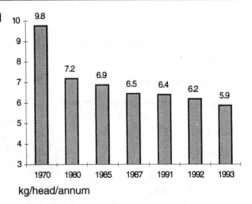

kg/head/annum

 ### KEY ASSESSMENT QUESTIONS (top third)

	Lowland		Upland
Nº lambs reared per ewe	152		141
Nº lambs born	160		153
Stocking rate / ha	12.6	(overall grassland)	110.6
Gross margin / grass ha	£562	lowland	£548
Output / ewe	£44.64		£51.68
Replacement rate	20%		

PRODUCTION

The EU sheepmeat regime supports the production of meat only. One premium scheme exists- annual ewe premium for breeding ewes (£19.25/head). (see 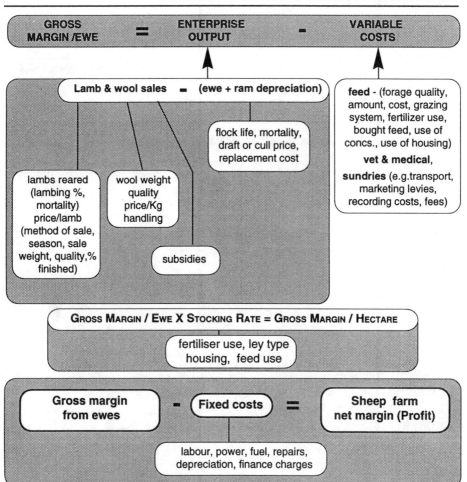)

FACTORS AFFECTING SHEEP PROFITABILITY

GROSS MARGIN /EWE	**=**	ENTERPRISE OUTPUT	**-**	VARIABLE COSTS

Lamb & wool sales **-** (ewe + ram depreciation)

feed - (forage quality, amount, cost, grazing system, fertilizer use, bought feed, use of concs., use of housing)

flock life, mortality, draft or cull price, replacement cost

vet & medical,

sundries (e.g.transport, marketing levies, recording costs, fees)

lambs reared (lambing %, mortality) price/lamb (method of sale, season, sale weight, quality,% finished)

wool weight quality price/Kg handling

subsidies

GROSS MARGIN / EWE X STOCKING RATE = GROSS MARGIN / HECTARE

fertiliser use, ley type housing, feed use

Gross margin from ewes	**-**	Fixed costs	**=**	Sheep farm net margin (Profit)

labour, power, fuel, repairs, depreciation, finance charges

Most lowland and upland farms have sheep along with other enterprises - especially cereals or cattle, and so it is not possible to allocate fixed costs to any one enterprise

PRODUCTION

THE PRODUCTION CYCLE - A SPRING LAMBING FLOCK

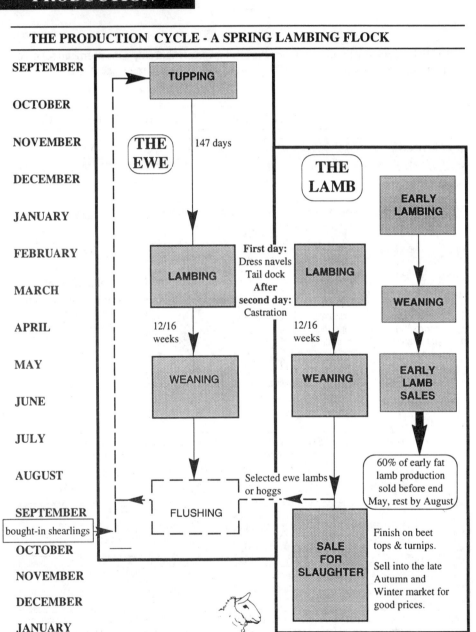

SEPTEMBER

OCTOBER

NOVEMBER

DECEMBER

JANUARY

FEBRUARY

MARCH

APRIL

MAY

JUNE

JULY

AUGUST

SEPTEMBER

bought-in shearlings

OCTOBER

NOVEMBER

DECEMBER

JANUARY

TUPPING

THE EWE

147 days

THE LAMB

EARLY LAMBING

First day: Dress navels Tail dock **After second day:** Castration

LAMBING

LAMBING

WEANING

12/16 weeks

12/16 weeks

WEANING

WEANING

EARLY LAMB SALES

60% of early fat lamb production sold before end May, rest by August

Selected ewe lambs or hoggs

FLUSHING

SALE FOR SLAUGHTER

Finish on beet tops & turnips.

Sell into the late Autumn and Winter market for good prices.

PRODUCTS

Meat   Lamb and mutton.

Lamb   Light (8-12.5 kg)/standard (13-17.5 kg), medium (18-20.5 kg) or heavy (21-26.5 kg) lambs under 1 year old.

Mutton   From 2 - 3 year old wether or ewe sheep sold as large carcasses needing careful hanging to ensure flavour and tenderness.

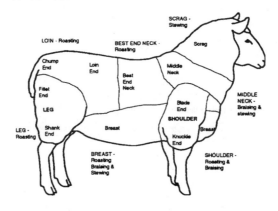

Wool   Returns from wool amount to approximately 5-10% of total returns per sheep. Hence it is often regarded as a by-product.

Milk   There are only approximately 6000 ewes in the UK kept for dairying.   Most is processed into cheese or yogurt.

MARKET OUTLETS

i   Exports

There has been considerable expansion in exports of sheepmeat in recent years. About 35% of all sheepmeat produced was exported. This was a firm market due to currency advantages but is now going down. Live exports have risen to 1,9 million head.

Exports '000 tonnes (1993)	
France	5.4
Bel/Lux	9.3
West Germany	2.1
Third countries	9.6

MARKETING

ii Livestock auctions

Still the most popular means of marketing lamb.

iii Deadweight system

Lambs are consigned direct to the place of slaughter. They are certified or rejected for variable premium as carcasses, and at the same time can be classified for conformation and fat cover.

Payment is usually based on weight and M.L.C. classification, although prices may vary from one wholesaler to another according to individual trade requirements. Farmers may produce lambs on contract to a central sheep marketing group aiming to meet specific market quality and quality requirements.

iv Wool marketing

All UK wool is sold to the British Wool Marketing Board. Most farmers receive less than this owing to deductions for contamination, broken fleeces, etc. Prices will remain very low as Australia withdrew (with NZ) wool pice support.

> **Average wool income = £1.30 - £2.05 per ewe.**

Levies

A levy of **52p** per lamb sold is payable to the M.L.C. This levy contributes to the funding of the Lamb Promotion Council. The **Lamb Promotion Council** is a body which represents producers, processors and retail interests. It is responsible for all domestic activities in lamb marketing and promotion.

PRICE SUPPORT

EU Sheepmeat Regime

Supports the production of meat only (therefore excludes Wool, Milk, Skins). **Aim** is to achieve a single community price for sheepmeat.

Annual ewe premium based on the number of breeding ewes in the flock.

Current value:lowland producers - approximately £19.25 per ewe.

Hill producers (in less favoured areas) - approximately £24.32 per ewe

Headage limits of 1000 in Less Favoured Areas and 500 elsewhere.

MARKETING

i   The variable premium scheme has been phased out.

ii Annual premium payments has increased to help offset this.

PRICES OVER A YEAR

Finished lamb prices 1993/4

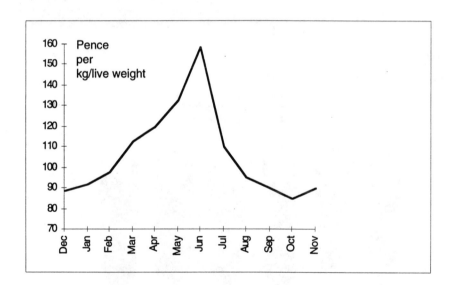

MARKETING

CARCASS CLASSIFICATION

The M.L.C. (Meat and Livestock Commission) classification scheme defines standards for the British meat industry to aid better marketing. This service provides a sound basis for meat traders to describe carcasses using common language. For sheep this is based on **fatness** and on **conformation**.

Fatness

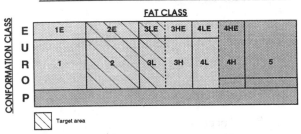

In **live lambs**, fat levels are assessed by handling over the loin and dock.

Conformation

Lambs with good conformation have:

thick loins
compact shoulders
thick, round legs

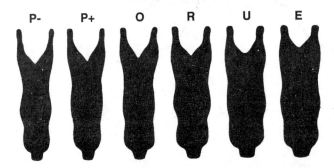

P-   P+   O   R   U   E

Killing out percentage is about 48% and this varies according to **breed, age, nutrition, sex.** The higher the killing out % the better the returns on the sheep. Of major importance here is the breed of sheep.

BREEDS & SYSTEMS

There are over 50 native UK breeds. Recently, there has been a rise in use of imported breeds. Listed below are just some of the more common examples.

Breeds

Hillbreeds

Small, alert, hardy; excellent mothering instinct with coarse wool. Examples are: Scottish Blackface, Welsh Mountain, Cheviot, Swaledale, Speckledface.

Longwool breeds

Used for crossing. Large bodied, high rate of twinning. Examples are: Blue Faced Leicester, Border Leicester, Bleu de Maine, Cambridge.

Halfbreeds (Longwool ram X hill ewe)

Medium sized, good mothers, milk well, good rate of twinning, easily managed. Examples are: Mule, Greyface, Welsh/Scottish Halfbred, Masham.

Terminal sire breeds

High growth rates, good conformation, excellent meat qualities, fine wool. Examples are: Suffolk, Texel, Hampshire, Dorset Down, Charolais

Breed Improvement

i   M.L.C. pedigree recording scheme

Selection indices are calculated for members. These are based on

> **birth weights**
> **growth rates**
> **ultra sonic scanning for fat and muscle depth**

ii Group breeding schemes

Members pool superior ewes into a nucleus flock, which produces superior rams for use in the members flocks e.g. Welsh Mountain Scheme to improve ewe size (CAMDA).

iii Imported breeds

The last 15 years has seen increased use of continental breeds e.g. Charolais, Texel, Bleu de Maine. Most of these have been used as terminal sires, improving conformation and lean content.

BREEDS & SYSTEMS

iv Artificial breeding techniques

As yet, little use has been made of techniques such as artificial insemination and embryo transplanting, due to variability of results achieved so far. However, it is expected that in the future these techniques will be improved and become more widely used.

SYSTEMS

Hills

Pure hill breeds used.

Products:
wethers plus unwanted ewe lambs sold as **stores**. Hill ewes after 3 to 4 lamb crops sold as **"Draft ewes"**.

Lambing date:
late April

Uplands

Draft ewes crossed with longwool rams.

Products:
wethers may be sold finished or as **stores**, ewe lambs or **shearling** ewes sold as **halfbred** (crossbred) breeding females to lowland producers.

Lambing date:
late March/Early April

Texel

Lowlands

Crossbred ewes mated with terminal sires.

Products:
finished lamb.

Lambing dates:
vary widely e.g.

Early lambing January/February aim to finish lambs for sale during period of high prices (April/May).

Late lambing late March/Early April aim to store lambs through Summer/Autumn and finish them during Winter on forage crops (e.g. turnips, swedes) or arable by-products (sugar beet tops).

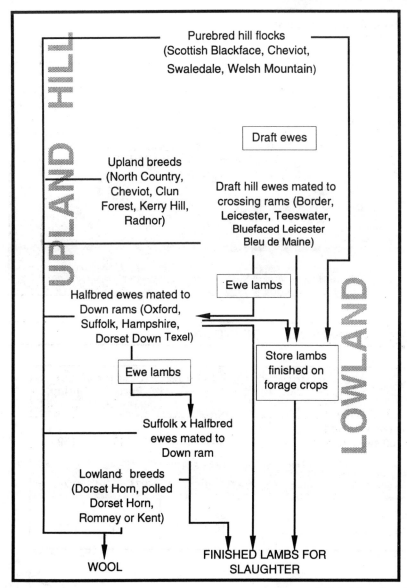

Source: Adapted from Speedy 'Sheep Production,Science into Practice'

BREEDS & SYSTEMS

UK SHEEP BREEDING SYSTEM

Scottish
Blackface

Beulah

Suffolk

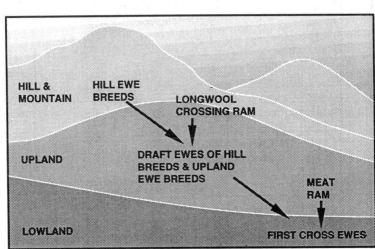

KEY ASSESSMENT QUESTIONS

	Hill/Upland	Lowland	
		Early lambing	Spring lambing
No. of lambs reared (per 100 ewes to ram)	141	149	152
Lamb sales (per ewe)	£33.99	£71.12	£39.70
Stocking rate (ewes per ha)	10.6	15.4	12.3

KEY ASSESSMENT QUESTIONS

		Lowland	Upland
Stocking rate (ewes/ha) At grass & forage		12.3	10.6
N fertiliser	per ha (kg)	· 79.00	41.00
Concentrates	per ewe (£)	6.94	6.05
	per lamb (£)	1.78	0.35
Forage costs	per ewe (£)	6.36	4.76

NUTRITION

Sheep are true **ruminants**. For most of their diet they are dependant on:

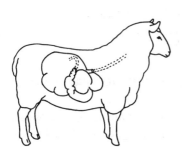

pasture	(grass & legumes)
forage crops	(e.g. turnips, swedes, rape, kale)
conserved forage	(hay & silage)

In arable areas sheep are often used to consume arable by-products, such as:

> sugar beet tops
> brassica waste
> "green" stubble

Concentrate feeds may be used to varying degrees depending on the breeding system and other available feeds.

FEEDING AIMS

The Ewe

The ewe is fed chiefly according to the stage of production cycle:

NUTRITION

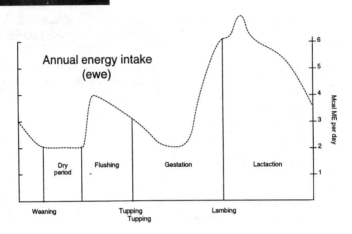

Annual energy intake (ewe)

Post Weaning

Feed is restricted to reduce milk pressure and lower the risk of mastitis. Once dried-off ewes are fed according to body condition:

Thin ewes - given preferential grazing to recover condition for mating;

Fat ewes - feed may be restricted to lose condition prior to mating.

Mating

At mating all ewes & tups should be in good condition **FIT BUT NOT FAT** (Condition Score 3 to 3.5).

2-3 weeks before mating, ewes (except hill ewes) will be "**flushed**" to increase fertility. This is done by moving ewes onto a higher plane of nutrition. (eg. grass reseed, silage aftermath or forage crop).

It is important to maintain ewe condition during the 1st month of pregnancy to ensure embryo survival.

Pregnancy

During the final 6 weeks of pregnancy 70% of foetal growth occurs, this, coupled with a reduction in the ewes appetite/intake often leads to a need for supplementary feeding, especially if twins/triplets are being carried.

e.g. twin bearing lowland ewe being fed moderate quality hay.

NUTRITION

Ration

	Concentrates kg/ewe/day	Hay(kg)
6-4 weeks pre-lambing	0.3	1.4
4-2 weeks pre-lambing	0.6	1.2
2 weeks pre-lambing	0.9	0.9

A suitable concentrate would have: ME of11-13 MJ/kg DM; Crude Protein 14-18%. It would also include minerals and vitamins e.g. typical home mixed ration:-

30%   Rolled oats
20%   Rolled barley
20%   Sugar beet pulp
16%   Soya bean meal
12%   Micronised beans
2%   Minerals/vitamins
(Cost = approximately £130/tonne)

Lactation

Milk yield and quality is very important for lamb growth up to 8 weeks.

Ewes are often turned out onto spring grass enabling concentrate feeding to be terminated quickly (3-4 weeks). Mangolds are often fed to lactating ewes as a milk stimulant.

Feeding Lambs

Pre-weaning

The young lamb lives on milk. As the lamb grows its rumen develops, and becomes adapted to digesting solid food. Rumen development may be accelerated by early access to solid feeds.

For intensive rearing, lambs may be weaned at 4-6 weeks. Traditionally lambs are weaned at 12-16 weeks.

Creep feeding

This is when lambs, still suckling, are given access to concentrates (usually high-17%/ 18% - crude protein). The feed is placed behind a restrictive barrier which prevents access to ewes. Creep feeding is only desirable where a sufficient number of the lambs will be finished early, and therefore be sold at a high price.

NUTRITION

Post Weaning

Weaned lambs are very susceptible to worm infection and should be moved onto:

(i) clean pasture:
a fresh re-seed, clover content 30% - 40% for fast growth
silage/hay aftermath
pasture not grazed by sheep in the previous year.

(ii) forage crops:
roots e.g. turnips
leafy e.g. kale, rape

CROPS FOR AUTUMN AND WINTER LAMB FEEDING

	Sowing date	Period of use	Lamb grazing days/ha*
Grass aftermath		July - Sept.	1000
Sugar beet tops		Oct. - Dec.	1500 - 2000
Rape	June - July	Oct. - Dec.	2000 - 3000
Stubble turnips	July - Aug	Nov. - Feb.	1000 - 4000
Swedes	April - May	Nov. - April	5000 - 10000

* The number of lamb grazing days is the stocking rate (lambs/ha) x the number of days each lamb spends on the crop.

For example, if the carrying capacity is 4000 lamb grazing days/ha, this may be utilized by 40 lambs for 100 days or 100 lambs for 40 days.

Occasionally cereal based concentrates may be fed (at about 0.25 kg/day) in order to finish lambs for market.

TARGET GROWTH RATES - LAMBS

Up to weaning	3000g / 400 g/day
Post weaning	50g / 250 g/day

INTRODUCTION

Greater profitability in sheep in recent years has led to greater intensification especially in lowland flocks. The use of Winter housing as well as higher flock densities has led to an increase in disease problems (watery mouth, etc.).

FACTORS AFFECTING SHEEP HEALTH

Nutrition

Lack of proper nutrition can lead to metabolic disorders (e.g. pregnancy toxaemia) and may also leave sheep prone to other health problems (e.g. hypothermia in lambs).

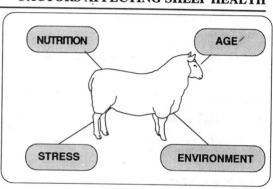

Environment

Certain environments provide a great risk of infection e.g. pasture contaminated with worm larvae, dirty lambing pens, etc.

Stress

This can be caused in many ways e.g. malnutrition, overcrowded housing, too long spent in transport, etc.

Age

Young lambs are generally more susceptible to disease and parasites.

MOST COMMON CAUSES OF ILL-HEALTH

Metabolic Disorders

Pregnancy toxaemia (twin lamb disease) lack of energy in twin/triplet-bearing ewes just before lambing.

Hypomagneseamia (staggers)   lack of magnesium in lactating ewes.

Swayback   lack of copper in pregnant ewes which affects the lambs.

HEALTH

External Parasites

These are organisms which attach themselves to and feed through the skin of sheep often causing intense irritation and stress, for example:

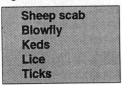

All of these are controlled by **dipping**.

Sheep scab
Blowfly
Keds
Lice
Ticks

Internal Parasites

These often have complex life cycles. They are picked up from the pasture as infectious larvae.

e.g. Stomach and intestinal worms (such as Nematodirus and Ostertagia)

Tapeworm
Liverfluke
Lungworm

These are controlled by grazing on clear pasture and/or dosing with Anthelmintics.

Bacterial/Viral Infections

There are many of these and they are fairly localised. The following are probably the most widespread:

i Clostridia infections*

E.g. pulpy kidney and tetanus are the most common of these infections picked up by grazing or through a cut in the animal's skin.

ii Pasteurella infections*

Many strains exist: T types associated with septicaemia in lambs between 6 - 9 months of age and in late autumn/winter; A types associated with pneumonia in adult sheep and septicaemia in lambs up to 6 weeks old.

iii Orf*

A highly contagious virus (caught by humans) which causes outbreaks of sores around mouth, feet and udders of sheep, often at lambing. Treatment is time consuming and costly. A live vacine exists for its control.

iv Infectious abortion*

Several organisms cause this, the most common types of abortion being Enzootic and Toxoplasma. Vital that at the first signs of outbreak, samples of aborted material is sent for typing at a veterinary laboratory.

HEALTH

v Footrot*

Common to most lowland flocks. It is a chronic condition which if untreated can lead to severe lameness and require the animal to be culled. Prevent by regular foot trimming and foot bathing in zinc sulphide or formaldehyde solutions. A vaccine is also available.

vi Coccidia

An infection which causes severe scouring and loss of condition in young lambs at or just after lambing. Hygiene is best form of prevention as treatment is costly.

vii Scrapie

A disease affecting the nervous system usually only seen in sheep 2 - 5 years old. Treatments are often ineffective and prevention by careful selection of replacements from 'scrapie-free' flocks .

viii Maedi visna

A kind of pneumonia, usually only seen in sheep 3 - 4 years old. Treatments are ineffective and prevention by careful selection of replacements. Rams for instance can be purchased from 'M.V. accredited' flocks.

* For most of these there are now effective vaccines available.

PROBLEMS ASSOCIATED WITH LAMBING

Lambs	Ewes
Hypothermia	Prolapse
Watery mouth	Lambing sickness
E. Coli scours	Metritis

Note: a lot can be done to avoid these by ensuring:

- ☛ proper feeding of ewe
- ☛ adequate colostrum intake by lamb (200 - 250 ml within first 6 hours)
- ☛ sensible vaccination programme
- ☛ navel spraying at birth with iodine solution

HEALTH

- clean lambing pens
- Adequate hygiene standards
- protection from harsh environmental conditions

ROUTINE HEALTH CARE

Vaccinations

These involve a preliminary course of 2 injections, normally 4-6 weeks apart, followed by a booster dose, usually given annually prior to the expected time of rise (e.g. prior to lambing). Vaccines are used to protect against:

> **clostridia infections**
>
> **pasteurella infections**
>
> **e. coli infections**

Antibodies produced by the ewe in response to the vaccine are passed to the lambs in the colostrum. This provides passive immunity to lambs which lasts about 10-12 weeks.

Worming

Ewes are normally wormed twice a year, at **lambing** and **flushing**.

Lambs are usually wormed first at about 8 weeks old then at 3-4 week intervals until weaning onto hay/silage aftermath, roots, etc.

Type of anthelmintic used will depend on level and type of infection expected, although it is recommended that the type of anthelmintic used is changed annually to avoid worm resistance.

Dipping

Lowland flocks dip in early summer to give Blowfly protection. Hill flocks may dip regularly throughout the Summer to control ticks.

HEALTH

Miscellaneous Preventative Measures

Foot bathing using 5% formalin or 10% zinc sulphate protects against foot infections such as scald and footrot.

Other measures include **correct feeding** (see |⬤|); **Suitable housing** (see 🏠). **Lambing hygiene:** use of clean bedding, navel dipping, clean equipment, etc. can minimise infections to lambs. **N.B.:** It is very important to observe the correct **withholding period** between administration of a medicine and slaughter for meat.

SHEEP AND GOAT HEALTH SCHEME

These are run by the Ministry. This is principally concerned with a viral disease caused by Maedi visna. Member flocks may achieve '**accredited**' status following 2 clear blood tests. In addition a monitoring service is available for:

> **enzootic abortion**
> **scrapie**
> **jaagsiekte**

NOTIFIABLE DISEASES

Outbreaks of the following diseases must be notified immediately to the Police or Government Department concerned:

> **sheep scab**
> **foot and mouth**
> **anthrax**

LEGAL HEALTH REQUIREMENTS

Medicine Record Book

Requires that the farmer keep up to date information about all medicines purchased and used on the farm. Failure is liable for a fine of up to £2000 .

HEALTH

Movement Register

The details (if any) of movement of any sheep to or from any premises must be recorded in a "Form of a record". Most farmers use the standard movement register book. Entries are to be made in ink or indelible pencil within 36 hours after the movement. Records are then required to be kept for one year. Fines of £500 - £600 for failure to keep proper records are quite common.

LEGAL ASPECTS

Welfare code

A new code came into force in September 1989 (M.A.F.F. leaflet 705).

Castration of lambs

Use of rubber rings is restricted to first week of the animal's life. Only a Veterinary Surgeon is allowed to castrate a ram over 3 months of age. Castration / tail docking must be done by an operator who is over 18 years of age unless supervised by a qualified vet.

Tail docking of lambs

Use of rubber ring is restricted to the first week of the animal's life. Sufficient tail must be left to cover:

> **vulva of female**
>
> **anus of male**

Tail docking must be done by an operator who is over 18 years of age unless supervised by a qualified vet.

Code For The Use Of Medicines

i **Source** - obtain products only from Veterinary Surgeons or registered Agricultural Merchants.

ii **Storage** - Store at correct light and temperature. Some products must be locked away. Always check expiry date prior to use.

iii **Records** - enter information in Annual Health Book.

iv **Withholding period** - the stated period between treatment and date of slaughter should always be observed to avoid residues in meat for human consumption.

HOUSING

WINTER HOUSING

Although there are still many hill flocks and a few late lambing lowland flocks that lamb outdoor, the majority of flocks now lamb indoors. Flocks are brought inside as soon as the climate or feed situation dictates, and are usually kept in until after lambing.

Advantages And Disadvantages Of Winter Housing

ADVANTAGES	DISADVANTAGES
improved supervision leading to fewer lamb losses	risk of disease spread e.g. pneumonia, footrot
better control of feed	extra feed cost
pasture protected from winter poaching	capital cost of the building
	requirement for bedding.
higher stocking rate obtained	

Space Requirements For Ewe

	Floor space	Trough space
60 kg Ewe	0.9 m²	45 cms
75 kg Ewe	1.2m²	50 cms

Other Requirements

- Fresh water
- Good lighting
- Good ventilation
- Draught free

- Clean bedding
- Adequate passage ways
- Mothering pens for ewes and lambs

Within the house, ewes should be penned in batches of up to 50 according to:

expected **lambing date,** or
number of lambs carried.

HOUSING

Types Of Housing

    i Empty granary, potato store etc.

    ii Converted farm building

    iii Purpose built house

Cost Of Purpose Built Housing

Plastic tunnel	£18/ewe
Pole barn	£35/ewe
Steel framed barn	£80/ewe

Costs vary widely according to materials used and how it is built.

HANDLING SYSTEM

A well designed handling system is essential to good sheep management. A shepherd can work far more quickly and efficiently if he is provided with good handling facilities.

Systems may be based on a permanent site or portable. Portable sites can be transported to the sheep and are now common where sheep are scattered over a wide area. There is no ideal layout but the principles are common to all situations.

General Principles

> **Site- central to area occupied by flock**
> **Free draining**
> **Slightly sloping**
> **Near water supply**
> **Accessible to metalled road**

Long, narrow shapes and funnels encourage sheep to flow. Sheep will readily move towards another sheep that they can see. Sheep are distracted if they see sheep to the side of the direction they are required to move.

A TYPICAL SHEEP HANDLING SYSTEM

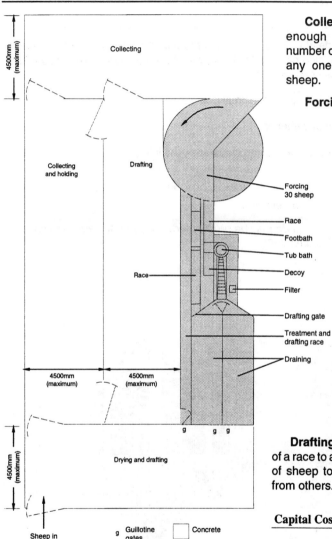

Collecting pen should be big enough to hold the maximum number of sheep to be handled at any one time. Allow 0.5m² per sheep.

Forcing pen allow sheep to be forced into face dip, footbath, etc. Usually circular or funnel shaped.

Drafting race allow sheep in single file. **Treatment race** allows sheep 3 - 4 wide for drenching, infecting, etc.

Footbath either narrow in the race to enable sheep to walk through formulin, or larger baths for zinc sulphate.

Dip essential for dipping to control scab, ticks, flies, etc. Usually 1000 - 3000 litre capacity.

Drafting gate placed at the end of a race to allow individual or groups of sheep to be drafted (separated) from others.

Capital Costs Of A Handling System

This varies greatly according to size, materials used, etc. The range should be £1500 - £6000.

HOUSING

 LEGAL ASPECTS

The Sheep Welfare Code

While this is only a code of practice it has the approval of Parliament. Anyone found breaking the code and causing distress to sheep, may be prosecuted. The code takes account of the basic needs of sheep viz:

☞ freedom from thirst, hunger and malnutrition

☞ appropriate comfort and shelter

☞ prevention/diagnosis and treatment of disease and injury

☞ freedom from fear

☞ freedom to display normal behaviour

Anyone found breaking the code may be prosecuted. A new code came into force in September 1989 (M.A.F.F. leaflet 705).

REPRODUCTION

KEY ASSESSMENT QUESTIONS

	Hill/Upland	Early lambing Lowland	Spring lambing Lowland
		FLOCK TYPE	
Ewes per ram	41	40	40
Barren ewes %	5	4	5
Lambs born alive*	146	158	160
Lambs born dead*	5	9	10
Lambs reared*	141	149	152
* Per 100 ewes to the ram			

KEY FACTS

Age of sexual maturity	6 months
Length of pregnancy	147 days
Length between heat periods	16 days
Duration of heat	2 days
Litter size	1-3 lambs

Note: ewes will only take the ram in Autumn/Winter. The exception being the Dorset Horn/Polled Dorset.

THE BREEDING YEAR

Culling

After weaning and the ewes have "dried off", they will be inspected and any not fit for a further breeding season will be removed (culled). Possible reasons for culling:

> **mastitis**
> **broken mouth**
> **chronic lameness**

Average annual culling rate = 20%

REPRODUCTION

Purchase Of Replacements

Usually takes place at Autumn breeding stock sales.

Females are usually purchased as **Shearlings** although some farmers breed from well-grown **ewe lambs**.

Expected cost:	Shearlings £75	Ewe lambs £50

(varies widely according to breed type, locality, demand, condition, etc.)

Males are usually purchased as Shearlings although some farmers buy well-grown ram lambs.

Expected cost:	Shearling £275	Ram lamb £175

Careful inspection of breeding rams, before purchase, is important especially for faults in legs, feet and mouth.

Flushing

This is the practice of **increasing fertility** by putting ewes onto a higher plane of nutrition (see |●|) It is not practised in hill flocks where the aim is for 1 lamb per ewe.

Introduction Of Teaser

A **teaser** (vasectomised ram) may be introduced to the flock about 16 days prior to entry of tups.

Reasons:

brings ewes into heat
synchronises heat/lambing

Tupping

Always keep enough rams to allow resting due to lameness, infertility, etc. Rams feet should be maintained in good order prior to and throughout tupping. Use of a colour crayon or paste allows monitoring of tup performance and planning of lambing management.

Scanning

The technique of ultrasonic scanning is now commonly used during mid-pregnancy of lowland flocks. It can be used with 99% accuracy to identify barren ewes, and with less accuracy can identify the number of lambs carried.

OUTSIDER'S GUIDE

REPRODUCTION

Lambing

Success depends on 3 main areas:

> **regular, careful observation**
>
> **provision of a suitable environment**
>
> **strict hygiene**

Weaning

Usually occurs when lamb 12 - 16 weeks old. Lamb should be weaned onto worm-free pasture, roots, etc.

ARTIFICIAL CONTROL OF BREEDING SEASON

Progesterone Sponges	PMSG
Implanted into the ewes vagina, will prevent heat until removal after 14 days. Used to sychronise heat.	Intramuscular injection at removal of progesterone sponges. Used to advance the breeding season and/or raise fertility.
A.I.	**Embryo Transplants**
Used in conjunction with sponges and PMSG. Not widely used owing to expense and problems in the conception rates.	A few pedigree breeds only are using E.T. but expensive and variable results have been reported.

FACTORS AFFECTING PRODUCTION

Age of ewe	Ewe lambs have lower fertility
Breed of ewe	See p 11
Condition of ewe	Condition score 3
Flushing	See p 16
Stress	Avoid during, and up to 4 weeks after tupping
Tupping date	Maximum fertility on ewe's 3rd/4th heat
Tup management	Condition score 3 Sound legs/feet 1 per 40 ewes

NOTES

PERFORMANCE

PHYSICAL PERFORMANCE

KEY ASSESSMENT QUESTIONS

	Lowland Spring	Lowland Early	Upland/Hill
Average flock size (ewes to ram)	537	250	738
Ewe to ram ratio	40	40	41
Ewes lambed (per 100 to ram)	90	91	91
Lambs reared (per 100 to ram)	152	149	141
Lambs retained/sold for breeding	10	6	23
Lambs sold finished	87	138	80
Lambs retained/sold for feeding	57	5	36
Stocking rate (ewes / hectare)			
Summer grazing	13.3	17.8	11.1
Overall grass and forage	12.3	15.4	10.6
N fertiliser / ha (kg)	79	50	41

Source: Adapted from the M.L.C. Sheep Year Book 1994

In the table above, the main physical performance indicators are in bold. These are **average** figures for sampled farms (421 lowland Spring lambing; 65 lowland early lambing; 149 upland and hill flocks). Better flocks owe their improved gross margins to the indicators summarised below.

%CONTRIBUTION TO TOP THIRD PERFORMANCE

	Lowland Spring lambing	Upland/Hill
Stocking rate	71	80
Flock replacement cost	9	13
Nº lambs reared (sold) /ewe	11	2
Feed and forage costs	4	-
Lamb price / head	6	2
Others	3	3

Source: Adapted from the M.L.C. Sheep Year Book 1994

PERFORMANCE

GROSS MARGIN ANALYSIS FOR FLOCK TYPES

	Upland/Hill	Lowland Early lambing	Lowland Spring lambing
Output (£ per ewe)			
Slaughter lamb sales	27.78	70.54	33.39
Lamb sales	33.99	71.12	39.71
Lamb valuations	14.88	4.20	14.31
Wool	1.62	2.05	1.91
Ewe premium and LDA subsidy	27.24	17.15	17.71
Gross receipts	77.51	94.52	73.64
Less Purchased Lambs	0.15	0.26	0.10
Ewe replacement cost	8.04	7.00	7.46
Output **(£ per ewe)**	**69.32**	**87.26**	**66.08**
Variable costs			
concentrates ewe	6.05	8.07	6.49
lamb	0.40	12.60	1.78
Purchased forage	0.28	1.10	0.81
Fertiliser	3.06	1.87	3.07
Other forage costs	0.18	0.41	0.41
Rented Grass Keep	1.20	1.80	1.21
Total feed & forage (£)	11.16	25.85	14.28
Vet & medicine	3.49	4.19	3.84
Other Cost	2.99	3.60	2.32
Total variable costs(£)	**17.64**	**33.64**	**21.44**
Gross margins per ewe (£)	**51.68**	**53.62**	**44.64**
Gross Margin per grass hectare	**548**	**863**	**562**
Gross margin per hectare	**548**	**826**	**549**

These are results from the **top one third** M.L.C. recorded flock for 199458

FIXED COSTS

The level of fixed costs vary considerably largely due to the level of fixed capital investment and subsequent depreciation / financial charges. An 'average' figure is likely to be around £25 to £35/ewe.

Fixed Costs Per Year

Examples of fixed costs £/ewe	Early Lambing	Lowland	Upland	Hill
Fixed Costs	£	£	£	£
Regular labour	12.5	16.2	12.7	9.5
Buildings & Land	9.0	9.4	6.6	3.8
Machinery & Other Costs	3.0	3.5	7.7	7.9
Interest on Livestock Working Capital	9.0	7.5	4.8	4.5
Total	**33.5**	**36.6**	**31.8**	**25.7**

Source A.D.A.S.

Contract charges	Ditching/ hedging only
Land maintenance	Tenants repairs & landlord type repairs as under a full repairing tenancy.
Sundries	Administration overheads - insurance, fees, office & telephone, subscriptions but excludes interest charges
New Farms	**New farm businesses may have 'rent charges' 40% to 70% higher than those indicated.**

PERFORMANCE

THE
OUTSIDER'S GUIDE
to
ANIMAL PRODUCTION
APPENDIX

1995 Edition

THE
OUTSIDER'S GUIDE
to
ANIMAL PRODUCTION
APPENDIX

1995 Edition

SUPPORT

Integrated Administrative & Control System (I.A.C.S)

Anti fraud measure to stop fraudulent claims for grants. I.A.C.S applies to Arable Area Payments, Beef Special Premium and Suckler Cow Premium. The system involves a form filling exercise which includes the submission of O.S. maps to M.A.F.F for identification purposes.

Other parts of the system will comprise of an identification system for each field, a system for identification and registration of certain animals. Penalties for late and inaccurate applications are severe.

Set Aside

A new set-aside scheme started as from the Autumn 1992 drilling. The payment for land set-aside was £253/ha in 1993, rising to £315/ha in 94/95. The amount of land to be 15% (18% on non rotational set-aside or flexible set-aside) of the land on which area payment can be claimed ie land used for wheat, barley, oats, rye, maize, oilseed rape, peas, field beans and linseed.

PRICE SUPPORT

Main Features

To compensate for a phased reduction in arable support prices, an area payments scheme has been introduced, paid directly to growers. To qualify for these aea payments, growers must set-aside 15% or 18% of their eligible land on which compensation will be paid.

Regional base area ceilings have also been introduced. If compensation claims exceed the regional base area, area payments for all growers in the region will be reduced proportionately, and growers must set-aside additional land the next year. In this way it is hoped to stabilise the EU farm budget.

Cereals	Wheat (inc. Durum), Barley, Oats, Rye, Triticale.
Oilseeds	Rapeseed, Sunflowers and Linseed.
Proteins	Dried Peas and Beans.

Land is not eligible if under permanent pasture (more than 5 years), woodland, non-agricultural use, S.S.I., nitrate sensitive area's etc. on 31st December 1991.

SUPPORT

Regional Payment Rates

These differ according to expected yield potential in differing areas of the UK e.g. in England for example where yields are expected to be greater due to a more favourable climate and better soil types, the level the level of compensation/ha is greater. UK is divided in 7 areas, England, Scotland, Wales and N.Ireland (LFA and non-LFA).

Regional Payment Rates 1994 - 96		
	1994/5	**1995/6**
Cereals	193.53	248.83
Oilseeds	436.88	
Proteins	385.45	
Linseed	481.06	
Set-aside	315.18	315.18
Additional Set-aside	219.69	219.69

NOTE: Details of the set-aside schemes and payment rates are in a state of flux as the Council of Ministers continue to iron-out the regulations. Level of payment can differ according to the value of the ECU.

Environmentally Sensitive Areas (ESAs)

Introduced in 1987 with the aim of conserving the British countryside. 44 areas have been designated ESAs covering 15% of agricultural land. Farmers volunteering are offered a ten year agreement. Annual payments vary between ESA's depending on amount of restrictions on farming activities. Payments of upto £400/ha may be paid.

Countryside Stewardship Scheme

A pilot scheme from the Countryside Commission available in England only, with only 7 target land types eligible including - heath, chalk/limestone grassland, waterside land, coastal areas and upland each contract is for a ten year contract. Payments from £20 to £250/ha plus £50/ha where public access is allowed.

Group Marketing Grant Scheme

This MAFF administered grant is to encourage the formation of new producer groups, and the improvement of existing groups. Scheme contributes 50% of the key management expenses in starting a group - feasibility studies, salaries, legal and training costs. In addition grants of 40 - 30 and 20% are available for the marketing cost for the first 3 years.

OUTSIDER'S GUIDE

Farm And Conservation Grant Scheme

Grants are made available under three main headings; land improvement and energy saving, waste handling facilities, environment and countryside.

Higher rates of grant (50%) generally apply in Less Favoured Areas (LFA's) and also where an improvement plan is submitted. Young farmers under the age of 40 may qualify for an additional 25% above standard rates.

Hedgerow Incentive Scheme

A voluntary scheme designed to both improve existing hedgerows and encourage new ones. Administered by the Countryside Commission. Agreements for 10 years and over for the whole farm.

Grant rates e.g. Gapping up £1.75/metre planted. Hedge laying £2/metre.

Countryside Access Scheme

Launched in September 1994 for set-aside land which is suited to new or unused public access will be eligible. £90/ha per 10m width access stops along or across fields. Larger areas will pay £45/ha. Land must be managed according set-aside rules.

Organic Aid Scheme

Started on 1st August 1994. Payments will be made for converting to organic farming over 5 years. Approval of the UK Organic Organisation is needed. Starts at £70/ha reducing to £25/ha at end.LFA's will receive only 20 % of grant.

Farm Woodland Premium Scheme

From April 1992 and replaces Farm woodland scheme which ended March 1992. Annual payments of up to £250/ha for planting on arable or improved grassland in Less Favoured Areas (LFAs) for 10 to 15 years according to woodland type. Payments of £60/ha for unimproved grassland in LFAs.

SUPPORT

BEEF

Intervention, Monetary Compensatory Allowances And Trade Agreements

Intervention is designed to take beef off the market when prices fall below a certain price. The EU will buy the beef and store it until prices improve.

Monetary compensatory allowances are designed to iron out distortions in currency rates between member states in the EU Intervention to be cut by 5% a year for 3 years.

Beef Special Premium (BSP)

Support paid directly to producers and is restricted to 90 male animals (at 10 and 22 months old) per year, when the animal is presented for slaughter. The payment is £67.50 in 1994 and £81 in 1995 per animal and is received about 6 weeks following sale.

Suckler Cow Premium (SCP)

An annual headage payment including milk producers producing below 60,000kg of milk (up to 10 animals). Animals must be kept for six months from the date the claim for S.C.P is lodged

There are two rates:

Non Less Favoured Areas: £56.34

Less Favoured Area: £59.64

For the next year a maximum of £85.50 is probable.

Hill Livestock Compensatory Allowances

These are paid at 2 levels to farmers in disadvantaged areas. The higher level on the more marginal (hill) farms £63.30 per cow and the lower level on somewhat more congenial situations, £46.86 per cow.

Integrated Administrative & Control System (I.A.C.S)

Anti fraud measure to stop fraudulent claims for grants. I.A.C.S applies to Arable Area Payments, Beef Special Premium and Suckler Cow Premium. The system involves a form filling exercise which includes the submission of O.S. maps to M.A.F.F for identification purposes.

Other parts of the system will comprise of an identification system for each field, a system for identification and registration of certain animals. Penalties for late and inaccurate applications are severe.

DAIRY

Quotas

The price of milk is supported through a national and EU quota scheme. The quota system (started in 1984) controlled the total supply of milk by the imposition of a production quota on each farm. The individual farm quota was the farm's 1983 production less 9%. Since then further reductions have been made. The effect of this constraint is to maintain prices received by those still in production. A cut of 1% in quota was made for 1992/1993. A further cut of 1% applies to the 1993/4 production year.

The basic Milk Target Price for the 1994-5 milk year is 21.6p/litre. The Intervention Price for butter is £2323.58 per tonne, and for skimmed milk powder it is £1567.49 per tonne.

Co-responsibility Levy

The milk target price is 21.96 p/litre, however there was a co-responsibility levy on milk sold to the M.M.B.s which was charged to the wholesale producers. This levy was abolished in April 1993.

The Super Levy

The super levy that is payable on milk produced over quota is 28.97 p/litre.

Other Payments

i   Hygiene bands (quality payment scheme on total bacteria count [T.B.C.]).

ii   Bulk milk cell count (quality scheme on herd mastitis levels).

iii   Seasonality payment for July to October, paid in December.

iv   Rolling fund payment (return of co-operative profits to farmers) paid in March.

SUPPORT

EGGS

There is no Government support for the UK egg producer.

PIGS

There is no Goverment support for the UK pig producer.

SHEEP

Price support is through the EU Sheep Meat Regime. This applies to live sheep and goats, fresh, chilled and frozen sheep meat and offals.

Basic Price

There is an EU basic price for sheep fresh and chilled carcasses set annually by the Council of Ministers. The level takes into account the current and projected sheep market situation, production costs and the situation in other meat sectors.

Private Storage Aid &Intervention

Periodically a Storage Subsidy is made available to take surplus carcasses off the market and temporarily into storage. This is hardly ever taken up. The scheme acts as a safety net to support the market should prices fall below a minimum level.

Hill Livestock Compensatory Allowances

These relate to the breeding and rearing of cattle and sheep in disadvantaged areas. Eligibility includes a farmer having more than 3 hectares on January 1st and continue to use that land for a period of 5 years. There is an overall upper limit of £62.48/ha and six ewes per hectare. Grants for cattle and sheep are added together.

Price Support

Stabilisers are a means of controling EU agricultural spending. A stabiliser scheme was introduced in May 1988 based on a threshold of 18m breeding ewes in Britain. For every 1% increase in numbers there is a reduction in the Basic price. In 1990 ewe numbers were still increasing. (1988 = 4.5%, 1989 = 3.8%, 1990 = 3.3%, 1991 = 8.1 %, 1992 = 0% increase in ewe numbers)

SUPPORT

Annual Ewe Premium

The annual ewe premium is based on the shortfall between the average market price and the basic price after allowing for the loss in variable premium (now abolished). This will be limited to the first 500 sheep in lowland flocks and the first 1000 head in Less Favoured Areas, additional ewes receiving only 50% of the rate.

Support Details For 1994/5

The ewe premium will increase to compensate for the loss in Variable Premium. An individual reference flock will be established for each producer in the base year (1989, 1990 or 1991) who is still producing.

Within this limit, or entitlement, full rate of Sheep Annual Premium will be paid on the first 1000 ewes per producer in the LFAs and the first 500 ewes per producer outside the LFAs. Beyond these limits half rates will be paid up to the producer's personal entitlement.

A national reserve has been created and used to enhance personal limits in special circumstances, for example producers part way through a development plan in the base year, or where base year numbers are abnormally low for some legitimate reason.

It is intended that entitlement is tradeable and that the land associated with the entitlement and continue to be used for keeping sheep. Trading entitlement without land is likely to result in a "tax" of up to 15% of entitlement being forfeited to the national reserve without compensation.

The definition of an eligible ewe for Sheep Annual Premium payments is amended to a female sheep which is at least twelve months old or has lambed on the qualifying date.

First instalment in September (40%), second instalment in December (60%) and the last payment in May 1995. I.A.C.S form to be used for the first time in 1994.

Headage Limit For Full Rate (Half Rate Thereafter)

1994 support	LFA	Non LFA
	1000	500
	19.25	19.25
	5.16	
Estimated Total	£24.41	£19.25

Hill Livestock Compensatory Allowances 1994 claimed by LFA farmers will be £5.75 (hardy breeding ewe, severely disadvantaged area); £3.00 (other breeds) and £2.44 (disadvantaged area).

OUTSIDER'S GUIDE

CONTACTS & TERMS

USEFUL REFERENCES

Agro Business Consultants	Agricultural Budgeting & Costing Book (latest edition)
Blowey R.W.	A Veterinary Book for Dairy Farmers
Cooper	Profitable Beef Production
Croston D & G Pollott	Planned Sheep Production
Eales E & Small J	Practical Lambing
English, Smith, Maclean	The Sow - Improving Her Efficiency
Esslemont R.J. ,Bailie J.H., & Cooper M.J.	Fertility Management in Dairy Cattle
Farming Press Ltd	T V Vet Sheep Book
Fell H	Intensive Sheep Management
Hardy & S Meadowcroft	Indoor Beef Production
Hughes P,Varley M	Reproduction in the Pig
Johnston R G	Introduction to Sheep Farming
M.A.F.F. Bulletin 33	Energy Allowances & Feeding Systems for Ruminants
McG. Cooper M. & Thomas R J	Profitable Sheep Farming
Meat & Livestock Commission	Pig Year Book 1994
Meat and Livestock Commission	Beef Yearbook
Milk Marketing Board (Publications)	Dairy Facts and Figures
MLC	MLC Sheep Yearbook 1994
Morris David	Practical Milk Production
Muldoon	Farm Vet Cattle Manual
National Cattle Breeders Assoc.	British Cattle
National Sheep Association	The Sheep Farmer (bimonthly periodical)
Nix J. , Wye College,	Farm Management Pocketbook (25th Edition)
Owen J. B	Cattle Feeding
Owen J. B	Sheep Production
Raymond et.al.	Forage Conservation & Feeding
Robert Young & Company Ltd'85	The Shepherd's Guide
Russell Kenneth	The Herdsmans Book
Sainsbury	Livestock Health & Housing
Sainsbury	Poultry Health and Management

CONTACTS & TERMS

Scottish Agricultural College Ltd	Monthly Economic Survey
Slater Ken	Principles of Dairy Farming
Slater Ken & Throup Gordon	Dairy Farm Business Management
Speedy A W	Sheep Production Science into Practice
Taylor D J	Pig Diseases
The Pig Veterinary Society Proceedings	Vol. 18
Thickett, Mitchell & Hallows	Calf Rearing
Thornton K	Outdoor Pig Production
Webster, John	Understanding the Dairy Cow
Wilkinson & Taylor	Beef Production from Grassland

USEFUL CONTACTS

A.D.A.S. Poultry Advisers	ADAS Nottingham, Chalfont Drive, Nottingham NG8 3SN (01602 425255)
AGENDA	Stoneleigh Park Pavilion, N.A.C. Stoneleigh, Kenilworth, Warwickshire CV8 2UG (01203 696996)
Agricultural Mortgage Corporation	AMC House, Chantry St, Andover, Hants SP10 1DD (01264 334344)
ATB Landbase Ltd	Stoneleigh Park Pavilion, N.A.C. Stoneleigh, Kenilworth, Warwickshire CV8 2UG (01203 696996)
Animal Health Distributors	41 Barrack Square, Martlesham Heath, Ipswich
British Association of Sheep Contractors	Cherry Croft Cottage, Compton, Winchester, Hants, SO21 2AS
British Cattle Breeders Club	Lavenders, Isfield, Nr. Uckfield, Sussex, TN22 5TX (0182575 356)
British Institute of Agricultural Consultants	Durleigh House, 3 Elm Close, Campton, Shefford Beds SG17 5PE (01462 813380)
British Sheep Dairying Association	Wield Wood, Alfresford, Hants. SO24 9RU (01420 563151)
British Wool Marketing Board	Oak Mills, Station Road, Clayton, Bradford, W. Yorks BD14 6JD (01274 882091)
British Pig Association	7 Rickmansworth Rd, Watford WD1 7HE (01923 34377)

CONTACTS & TERMS

Farming and Wildlife Advisory Group	The Lodge, Sandy, Bedfordshire SG19 2DL (01767 80551)
Food From Britain	417 - 418 Market Towers, New Covent Garden Market, London SW8 5N7 (0171 720 7551)
Health & Safety Executive	HM Agricultural Inspectorate, Baynards House, 1 Chepstow Place, London W2 4TF (0181 299 3456)
HMSO Publications Centre,	PO Box 276, London SW8 50T. (0171 622 3316)
De Montfort School of Agriculture	Caythorpe Court, Grantham Lincolnshire NG32 3EP (01400 72521)
Meat & Livestock Commission	P.O.Box 44, Winterhill House, Snowdon Drive, Milton Keynes MK6 1AX (01908 677577)
Milking Machine Manufacturers	Yorkings, Grange Park, Whitchurch, Ross-on-Wye, MR9 6EA. (01600 890597)
Ministry of Agriculture (M.A.F.F.)	3 Whitehall Place, London SW1A 2HH (0171 270 3000)
National Association of Agricultural Contractors (NAAC)	Huts Corner, Tilford Road, Hindhead, Surrey, GU26 6SF (01428 605360)
National Cattle Breeders Assoc.	Lawford Grange, Lawford Heath, Rugby, Warwick CV23 9HG (01788 565264)
National Farmers Union (N.F.U.)	Agriculture House, 22 Long Acre, London W1M 0AP (0171 325 5077)
National Office of Animal Health	3 Crossfield Chambers, Gladbeck Way, Enfield, Middlesex, EN2 7HF(0181 367 3131)
National Proficiency Test Council.	Tenth Street, National Agricultural Centre, (NPTC) Stoneleigh, Warwickshire CV8 2LG (01203 56132)
National Sheep Association,	The Sheep Centre, Malvern, Worcs, WR13 6PH (01684 892661)
Royal Agricultural Society of England	National Agricultural Centre, Stoneleigh, Warwickshire CV8 2LZ (01203 696969)
Specialist Consultants	Meat Quality: Nick Lynn, Block 2, Goverment Buildings Otley Road, Lawnswood, Leeds LS16 5PY (01532 611222)
Environment Specialists:	Dr. D. Charles, Dr. D Mercer. Systems Specialist: A. Elson.
Feeding Specialist:	R. Pugh. Block 7, Government Buildings, Chalfont Drive, Nottingham NG8 3SN. (01602 291191)

CONTACTS & TERMS

GLOSSARY

2-Tooth	maiden breeding ewe that is usually about 18 months old
Abattoir	slaughterhouse
Anaemia	lack of haemoglobin in blood
As Hatched - (A/H)	chicks are often sold as Ashatched meaning that they are literally that, no sexing has taken place and there should be approximately equal numbers of males and females.Battery cages for laying hens using steel mesh or timber and wire netting in stepped or vertical arrangements of 1 to 6 tiers
Barrener	an infertile cow. Sometimes applied to other animals; e.g. a ewe that has failed to conceive after mating
Battery	cages for laying hens using steel mesh or timber and wire netting in stepped or vertical arrangements of 1 to 6 tiers
Bovine	referring to cattle
Broiler	a chicken usually between the ages of 42-49 days of age.
Broken Mouthed Ewe	ewe with broken, worn or missing teeth
Brooding	term used to describe the early period in a chickís life and the provision of heat to keep chicks warm
Cade	orphan lamb
Calving interval (index)	interval between one calving and the next
Calving percentage	number of calves produced as a percentage of those mated
Candling	eggs are inspected in a bright light for cracks and other internal faults such as infertile eggs in breeding units which makes them unsuitable for sale or use
Cannibalism	pecking, possibly to death of other hens by hens, its incidence reducing with lower flock density
Cockerel	male chicken
Colostrum	first milk produced after calving
Coma	profound unconsciousness

OUTSIDER'S GUIDE

CONTACTS & TERMS

Concentrates	food supplying a high amount of energy and/or protein per unit weight
Conception	fertilisation of an egg by a sperm
Conformation	soundness of body. In carcases - amount of lean meat; shape
Cracks	about 10% of eggs are down graded to second quality because of cracks and are put in class C and can not be sold in shops but are used for processing
Deadweight	carcass (liveweight less offals)
Draft ewe	mountain ewe (4-5 years old) sold to upland farmers for crossing
Dry cow therapy	use of a slow release antibiotic which is injected into the udder through the end of the teat after the last milking at the end of lactation
Dry period	the 4 to 6 week rest from end of one lactation to next calving
Embryo	the developing young in the uterus
Ensiling	a method of storing grass or other crops by inducing a pickling of the material which must be stored without access to air or oxygen
Enzootic	relating to a disease in a particular area
Feed conversion ratio	ratio of feed consumed to weight of eggs or meat produced
Fibre	the part of plant feed made of cellulose which can only be digested by microbes
Finish	appearance of carcase, should be creamy white in colour caused by a layer of subcataneous fat or finish
Fixed costs	costs which cannot readily be allocated to a specific enterprise on a farm, or will not vary with small changes in the scale/output of the enterprise
Flushing	increasing the plane of the flock's nutrition prior to and throughout mating to ensure a high rate of ovulation
Food conversion efficiency	number of kilogrammes of food needed to produce one kilogramme of liveweight gain
Gestation	period during which a female is carrying its offspring in the uterus

CONTACTS & TERMS

Gimmer	maiden breeding ewe that is usually about 18 months old
Growth rate	speed of growth, usually quoted in gms/day
Hardiness	ability to withstand extremes of weather
Hardy	able to stand extremes of climate
Hatchery	birthplace of chicks
Heat (oestrus)	period during which a female will allow mating and ovulation takes place
Hen	after 12 months of lay a pullet becomes a hen
Hogg	young female lamb destined for breeding
Hoggett	store lamb destined for slaughter
HSE	Health and Safety Executive
Hybrid	a product of two or more pure lines which tend to exhibit hybrid vigour and is superior to any of its parents and today hybrids make up the commercial laying flock
Immunity	exempt - resistance to infection
Infection	invasion by disease causing agents
Intensive	allowing expression of full potential or reducing space (land) allowed
Intervention	a system by which produce is bought from farmers when markets are weak and stored for later sale
Killing Out %	deadweight as a percentage of liveweight. This increases with liveweight. With lambs this is usually 45% - 48%
Lactation	period during which an animal is producing milk, from birth of one calf / lamb etc. until the start of a rest or dry period before birth of the next offspring
Lactation	period when a female is producing milk
Layers	adult commercial hybrid chickens bred to lay white, tinted or brown eggs which produce most of the eggs for consumption
Lice	pale yellowish-brown insects found near the vent usually controlled through thorough cleaning the empty layer house
Liveability	number of birds remaining in a flock, usually expressed as a %

CONTACTS & TERMS

Mortality	number of birds in flock that die, usually expressed as a %
Liveweight	weight of the live animal
Lower Critical Temperature	temperature below which food is used to produce heat
Maintenance	portion of food required to give energy to operate all the body systems, i.e. to maintain life
Mastitis	infection of the udder
Metabolic	relating to metabolism i.e. the sum of all physical and chemical processes of the bodyís working
Milk solids	the fat, protein, lactose, mineral and vitamin constituents of milk
Mule	a crossbred ewe
Ovulation	release of ova (eggs) from the ovaries during the heat period particular sites.
Parasite	a living organism which lives off another living organism to the latter's detriment
Pesticides	any chemical which is used to kill, control or diminish not just insects but also weeds and diseases which challenge man, his crops, his domestic animals and his environment
Point of lay	the time at which pullets start laying usually 20 to 22 weeks
Post Brooding	Period in chickens life after brooding period a temperature of 21°C is usually adopted
Prolificacy	fecundity (reproductive productivity)
Pullet	female chicken from one day old up to 12 months when it becomes a hen
Roughage	a food high in fibre e.g. hay, straw
Rumen	the largest section of the stomach of cattle and sheep
Scour	diarrhoea
Service	mating
Slurry	a mixture of urine and faeces with or without the addition of water

CONTACTS & TERMS

Stocking rate	the number of hectares of land allocated to dairy, beef or sheep, including production of conserved forage divided by the average number of head in the herd in a year
Stress	an unwarranted expenditure of energy
Sub-clinical	symptoms are so slight that they escape notice
Suckler cow	cow which rears its calf for the whole of its lactation
Superchicken	a chicken, usually a male, grown to 49-70 days. Also known as Roasters and Capons, though the term capon strictly speaking refers to a male castrate which are no longer available
Tainted	flesh or eggs can be tainted by feed ingredients, wood preservative in the litter and storing eggs near to strong smelly substances
Teaser	a vasectomised ram
Tenant's capital	farm assets normal provided by tenants and includes livestock, machinery, crops in store, stocks, work in progress, cash and other assets needed to run a business
Theave	maiden breeding ewe that is usually about 18 months old
Tupping	mating
Vaccination	method of producing an active immunity against a specific infection
Variable costs	costs which can easily be allocated to a particular enterprise and vary directly with the size of the enterprise (feed, medicines, casual labour etc.)
Vice	undesirable habits such as feather pecking, vent pecking, cannibalism, etc.
Wether	castrated male sheep
Withdrawal time	time which must elapse between the last administration of a drug and slaughter
Working capital	assets required to finance the production cycle such as all variable cost items, plus labour, power costs etc.

OUTSIDER'S GUIDE

CONTACTS & TERMS

Animal Breeding & A.I, Embryo Transfer Companies

Avoncroft Cattle breeding centre	Bromsgrove, Wrocestershire (015127 31481)
Embryo and Semen World	Tostre House, Glascoed, Pontypool, Gwent. (01495 750954)
Genus Breeding Services	Thames Ditton, Surrey KT7 0EL (0181 398410)
Independent Stock Improvement	Lower Farm, Stoney Thoryze, Southam, Warwicks (0192 681 3634)

Building & Equipment Suppliers - All Livestock

Abacus	Sutton in Ashfield, Notts NG17 5FT
Alfred Cox (Surgical Ltd),	Edward Road, Coulsdon, Surrey, CR3 2XA
Aqua 2 Products	Amber Drive, Bailey Brook Industrial Estate, Langley Mill, Nottingham NG16 4BE. (01773 765316)
ARCH Ltd, Aisby	Grantham, Lincs.
Aston Equipment	4 Chase Road, Northern Way, Bury St Edmunds, Suffolk IP32 6NT (10284 70155)
Batchelor Farm Supplies	Winterbourne Kingston, Blandford, Dorset
Beechcroft	Pickhill, Thirsk, N. Yorkshire YO7 4JG
Bell Webster Concrete Ltd	Alma Park Rd, Grantham, Lincs
Big Dutchman GB Ltd	Sanders Lodge Indutrial Estate, Rushden, Northants, NN10 9BQ. (01933 55411)
C.F.P. Tuff Brand	Ruston Rd, Desborough, Kettering, Northants
Challow Fabrications Ltd.	9/10 Rectory Lane Trading Estate, Kingston,Bagpuize, Abingdon, Oxfordshire OX13 6AS
Collison Livestock Feeding Systems	Riverside Industrial Park, Catterall, Preston
E.B. Equipment Ltd	Redbrook, Barnsley, S York S75 1HR (01226 206896)
Gallagher	Henderson Livestock Equipment, Lyng Road, Wood Norton, E. Dereham, Norfolk NR20 5BJ
H.A.T	Unit 15, Reindeer Close, West Street, Horncastle, LIncs LN9 5AA (016582 6895)

CONTACTS & TERMS

Hanford Engineering Ltd	Piddlehinton, Dorchester, Dorset DT2 7TU
Harlow Houses	Long Whatton, Nr Loughborough, Leicestershire LE12 5DE. (0509 842561)
Industrial &Cladding Systems Ltd	Capital Valley, Rhymney, Gwent, NP2 5ET
J. Booth Engineering Ltd.	Ford Airfield Industrial Estate, Ford, Arundel, W.Sussex
J.A. & P.E. Wright	Brettenham Manor, Thetford IP24 2RP
Lindrick	Pocklington Industrial Estate, York Road, Pocklington, York
Lister Shearing Equipment Ltd,	Long Street, Dursley, Gloucs, GL11 4HR
Livestock Systems	Milbury Heath, Wotton under Edge, Gloucs. GL12 8QL
Maystead Developments Ltd	Fodens Old Foundry, Station Rd.,Elworth, Sandbach, Cheshire, CW11 9JG
Maywick (Hanningfield) Ltd	Rettenden Common, Chelmsford, Essex CM3 8HY (01245 400637)
Patchett Ltd RJ	Ryefield Works, Clayton Heights, Queensbury, Bradford, W. York BD13 1DS (01274 882331)
Peter Allen	The Wharf, Mill Street, Wantage, Oxfordshire OX12 9AR
Phillip Structures Ltd	Red Barn Drive, Hertford HR4 9NU
Probiotics International Ltd,	Milland House, Liphook, Hants
R. Tyler	Limes Farm, Hough on the Hill Grantham, Lincolnshire NG32 2BH
Ritchley Tagg Company,	Masham, Ripon, N. Yorks, HG4 4ES
Robinson Construction	Wincanton Close, Ascot Drive Industrial Estate, Derby DE2 8NJ
Rowland Bros.	Dunkirk, Aylsham, Norwich NR11 2BH
Strong Spec	Stradbroke House, 44 The Street, Brundall, Norwich NR11 6SU
Sturdy Stys	Factory in Wooler, Northumberland

CONTACTS & TERMS

DAIRY HERD RECORDING SERVICES AND SOFTWARE

DAISY	University of Reading, Dept. of Agriculture, Earley Gate, Reading, Berks., RG6 2AT (01734 67886)
Hunday Electronics	Samson Close, Killingworth, Newcastle Upon Tyne, NE12 0DX

FEED SUPPLIERS - ALL LIVESTOCK

A-One Feed Supplements	Tower House, Fishergate, York YO1 4UA
Alfred Cox (Surgical) Ltd	Edward Rd, Coulsdon, Surrey, CR3 2XA
B.O.C.M. Pauls Ltd	P.O. Box 39, 47 Quay Str., Ipswich, Suffolk IP4 1BX
Bibby Ltd	Adderbury, Banbury, Oxfordshire OX17 3HL
British Sugar Trident Feeds	PO Box 11, Oundle Road, Peterborough PE2 9QX
Colborn Dawes Ltd	Heanor Gate, Heanor Derbyshire DE7 7SG
Daisy Hill Pigs Ltd	Burstwick, Hull HU12 9HE
Dalgety Agriculture Ltd	180 Aztec West, Almondsbury, Bristol BS12 4TH
F.S.L. Bells Ltd	Corsham, Wiltshire,SN13 0QB (01249 712051)
Four-F Nutrition	Darlington Rd, Northallerton, N.Yorks DL6 2NW
George Palmer Ltd	Oxney Road, Peterborough, PE1 5YZ
J Bibby Agriculture Ltd	Head Office, Adderbury, Banbury, Oxon
Kemin (UK) Ltd	Becor House, Green Lane, Lincoln LN6 9DL (01522 514148)
Preston Farmers	County mill, Ruskington, Sleaford, Lincs.
Rumenco	Stretton House, Derby Road, Stretton, Burton on Trent, Staffs. , DE13 ODW
S C Associates Ltd	Sowerby, Thirsk, N. Yorks YO7 1HX
Trident Feeds	British Sugar, P.O. Box 11, Oundle Road, Peterborough, PE2 9QX (01733 63171)
Vetco Products	Waterclip Mill, Cranmore, Shepton Mallet, Somerset BA4 4RN
VOLAC Ltd	Orwell Works, Royston, Herts. SG8 5QX

CONTACTS & TERMS

HEALTH PRODUCTS - ALL LIVESTOCK

Antec International	Chilton Industrial Estate, Sudbury, Suffolk CO10 6XD
Battle Hayward & Bower Ltd	Crofton Drive, Allenby Road Industrial Estate, Lincoln
Bayer UK Ltd	Eastern Way, Bury St Edmunds, Suffolk, IP32 7AH
Beecham Animal Health	Beecham House, Great West Road, Brentford, Middlesex TW8 9BD (0181 560 5151)
Ciba Geigy Ltd	Whittlesford, Cambridge, CB2 4QT
Coopers Pitman-Moore	Crewe Hall, Crewe, Cheshire CW1 1UB
Crown Veterinary Pharmaceuticals	Minster House, Western Way, Bury St Edmunds, Suffolk, IP33 3SU
Cyanamid of Great Britain Ltd	Cyanamid House, Fareham Road, Gosport, Hampshire PO13 0AS (01329 224000)
Deosan Ltd	Weston Favell Centre, Northumberland, NN3 4PD
Duphar Ltd	Southampton SO3 4QH
Elanco Animal Health	Dextra Court, Chapel Hill, Basingstoke, Hampshire, RG21 2SY (01256 485079)
Fisons Pharmaceutical Division	12 Derby Road, Loughborough, Leics LE11 OBB
Hoechst (UK) Ltd	Walton Manor, Walton, Milton Keynes MK7 7AJ (01908 665050)
Intervet UK Ltd	Science Park, Milton Road, Cambridge CB4 4FP. (01223 420 221)
Jansen Animal Health Ltd	Grove Wantage, Oxford, OX12 ODQ
Leo Laboratories Ltd	Animal Health Division, Longwick Road, Princes Risborough, Aylesbury, Bucks HP17 9RR
M.S.D. Agvet	Hertford Rd, Hoddesdon, Herts, EN11 9BU
May and Baker	Dagenham, Essex, RM10 7XS (0181 592 3060)
Micro-Biologicals Ltd	Minster House, Western Way, Bury St Edmunds, Suffolk IP33 3SU. (01284 700145)
MSD Agvet Ltd	Hoddeson, Herts, EN11 9BU
Norbrook Laboratories (GB) Ltd	9 Mansfield Street, London W1M 9FH
Rappa Fencing Ltd	Stockbridge, Hampshire

CONTACTS & TERMS

Roche Products Ltd	Vitamin & Chemical Division,Broadwater Road, Welwyn Garden City, Hertfordshire, AL7 3AY (01707 328128)
Smith Kline Animal Health Ltd	Cavendish Rd, Stevenage, Herts SG1 2EJ
Sorex Ltd	Widnes, Cheshire WA8 8TJ
Upjohn Ltd	Agricultural Veterinary Division, Fleming Way, Crawley, West Sussex, RH10 2NJ (01293 31133)

PIG BREEDING STOCK

Seghers Hybrid	Grosvenor Mansions, Queen Str, Deal, Kent
Cotswold Pig Development Co Ltd	Rothwell, Lincoln LN7 6BJ
National Pig Development Co	Manor House, Beeford, Driffield, E Yorks YO25 8BD
Newsham, Hybrid Pigs	Musley Bank House, Malton, N. Yorks YO17 OTD
Norwich Pig Breeding Co (AI)	High House Farm, Little Melton, Norwich NR9 3PE
Pig Genetics (AI)	Skipton Old Airfield, Sandhutton, Thirsk, N. Yorks YO7 4EG
Pig Improvement Co Ltd	Fyfield Wick, Abingdon, Oxon OX13 5NA
Premier Pig Link HW	Holbein Farm, Great Eversden, Cambridge CB37
Rattlerow Farms	Hill House Farm, Stradbroke, Diss, Suffolk
J.S.R. Ltd	Southburn, Driffield, E Yorks

PIG RECORDING EQUIPMENT AND SYSTEMS

Easicare Computers Ltd	Upton House, Beeford, Driffield, E. Yorks YO25 8AF
H M Boot	Bleak House Farm, Aston, Nantwich, Cheshire CW5 8DS
Hylton Nomis	28 The Spain, Petersfield, Hants GU32 3LA
Logiporc	71 Castle Street, Salisbury SP1 3SP

CONTACTS & TERMS

Pig Champ	Pig Breeding Supply Co. LtdCheckendon, Reading, Berks RG8 0SP
Pigtales Ltd	Hill Top Farm, Main Street, Coniston, Hull HU11 4JR

POULTRY STOCK SUPPLIERS

Blue Barns Hatchery	West Acres, Pennyfine Rd, Sunniside, Newcastle upon Tyne NE16 5ER (0191 4887171/4102809)
Euribrid	Joice & Hill, South Raynham, Fakenham, Norfolk (01328 74216)
Farm Fresh (Hatchery) Ltd	132 Blackgate Lane, Tarleton, Preston, Lancs PR4 6UU (01772814081)
Hy-Line International	see Sappa Chicks (below)
I.S.A. Poultry Services Ltd	Green Road, Eye, Peterborough, Cambs PE6 7YP (01733 223333)
SAPPA PLC	Northern Way, Bury St Edmunds, Suffolk IP32 6NZ (01284 753161)
SAPPA Chicks	The Hatchery, Fornham All Saints, Bury St. Edmunds, Suffolk IP28 6JJ

SHEEP MANUFACTURERS OF POLYTHENE TUNNEL HOUSING

McGregor Polytunnel Ltd,	Soames Lane, Ropley, Hants SO24 OER
Polybuild Ltd & Netlon Ltd.	Unit 5C, Tewkesbury Industrial Centre, Delta Drive, Tewkesbury, Glos, GL20 8HD

SHEEP ARTIFICIAL INSEMINATION & EMBRYO TRANSPLANT

Coulthard Embryos Ltd,	Woodlea, Tattershall Road, Woodhall Spa, Lincs, LN10 6TP
Transgene McDougall	Barnfield Road, Forest Green, Nailsworth, Stroud, Glos, GL6 OEW

CONTACTS & TERMS